Innovative Software Engineering

Mastering Cross-Platform Application Development with Python, C#, and Modern Frameworks

THOMPSON CARTER

Table of Content

TABLE OF CONTENTS

Introduction

In today's fast-paced technological landscape, building applications that work seamlessly across multiple platforms has become a critical requirement for businesses and developers alike. The need to reach a wider audience, ensure consistent user experiences, and reduce the time and cost associated with developing separate applications for different platforms has made cross-platform development a key strategy in modern software development. Whether it's for mobile, desktop, or web applications, the ability to create cross-platform solutions can significantly increase efficiency, scalability, and reach.

This book, *Innovative Cross-Platform Development: Leveraging Python, C#, and Emerging Frameworks for Scalable Applications*, aims to equip developers with the knowledge, tools, and strategies necessary to master cross-platform development in today's diverse technological ecosystem. The focus is on helping you build high-quality, performant apps across multiple platforms using **Python, C#**, and the cutting-edge cross-platform frameworks available today.

What This Book Offers

Throughout this book, we'll explore the nuances of cross-platform development from its fundamental concepts to advanced techniques. Whether you are a beginner looking to get started with building cross-platform apps or an experienced developer seeking to deepen your expertise, this book offers insights and practical knowledge that will help you succeed in the field.

Here's what you can expect to learn:

- **Core Concepts of Cross-Platform Development**: We begin by defining cross-platform development, understanding its benefits, challenges, and the various frameworks and technologies that facilitate it. You will gain clarity on the differences between native, hybrid, and cross-platform approaches, helping you choose the right strategy for your project.

- **Cross-Platform Frameworks**: We dive deep into the world of frameworks such as **Flutter**, **React Native**, **Xamarin**, and **.NET MAUI**. Each framework has its own set of strengths and trade-offs. We'll guide you through how to use these frameworks to build efficient, maintainable, and user-friendly apps across various platforms, including mobile (iOS/Android), desktop, and the web.

- **Leveraging Python and C# for Cross-Platform Apps**: While some developers default to JavaScript or Swift for building mobile apps, Python and C# are powerful yet underappreciated languages in the cross-platform space. We will show you how Python, with frameworks like **Kivy**, **Flask**, and **Django**, and C#, with tools like **Xamarin** and **.NET MAUI**, can be used to build modern, cross-platform applications that can run on a variety of devices.

- **Advanced Techniques**: We will also explore advanced topics, such as **asynchronous programming**, **concurrency**, **design patterns**, **AI and machine learning integration**, and **IoT development**. These topics will help you optimize your applications for performance, scalability, and functionality, ensuring that they are robust and future-proof.

- **Real-World Examples**: Throughout the book, we will showcase real-world applications and case studies to help you understand how industry leaders are using cross-platform development. These examples will help you see the practical application of the concepts and techniques discussed in the book, giving you insights into how successful applications are built and maintained.

Why This Book is Important

The world of app development is rapidly evolving, with new platforms, tools, and libraries constantly emerging. Cross-platform development is no longer just a trend; it has become a necessity for developers who want to create applications that can run on a variety of devices without the overhead of maintaining separate codebases for each platform. By mastering the art of cross-platform development, you can future-proof your skills, expand your career opportunities, and create applications that deliver consistent and high-quality user experiences across multiple devices and operating systems.

This book emphasizes practical knowledge and hands-on learning. It's designed to give you both the theoretical foundations and the practical skills you need to build real-world, scalable applications. Each chapter is structured to help you build your understanding step by step, starting from the basics and moving toward more advanced topics. Whether you are a novice or an experienced developer, this book provides a clear, actionable path to mastering cross-platform development.

Who Should Read This Book?

This book is written for developers at all skill levels who are interested in learning or improving their cross-platform development skills. Whether you are:

- A **beginner** looking to dive into the world of cross-platform development and understand the core concepts and frameworks.
- An **intermediate developer** with some experience in native or hybrid development, seeking to expand your knowledge and learn new cross-platform tools and best practices.
- An **experienced professional** wanting to keep up with emerging technologies in Python, C#, and cross-platform frameworks, and to learn how to implement advanced techniques for building high-performance, scalable apps.

By the end of this book, you will not only have the technical expertise to build cross-platform applications using Python, C#, and popular frameworks, but you will also be equipped with the skills to tackle the challenges of real-world app development, from integration with cloud services to handling AI and machine learning features.

A Journey of Growth and Mastery

Cross-platform development is a continuously evolving field. The technologies and best practices of today may be obsolete tomorrow, but with the solid foundation this book provides, you'll be equipped to adapt and evolve. From learning the basics to mastering advanced techniques, this book will guide you on your journey to becoming a proficient cross-platform developer.

I invite you to embark on this journey with me, exploring the exciting world of cross-platform development. By the end of this book, you'll have a toolkit of skills that will enable you to create apps that can run seamlessly across platforms, providing valuable solutions to real-world problems and enhancing your career in the process. Let's get started!

CHAPTER 1

INTRODUCTION TO CROSS-PLATFORM DEVELOPMENT

What is Cross-Platform Development and Why It Matters?

Cross-platform development refers to the practice of creating software applications that can run on multiple operating systems (OS) or platforms with minimal modification. The goal is to write code once and have it function across different devices, operating systems, or environments such as Windows, macOS, Linux, Android, and iOS. This approach saves time, resources, and costs by eliminating the need to develop separate versions of an application for each platform.

For businesses and developers, cross-platform development means a broader audience reach, as apps can be distributed on multiple platforms simultaneously. This is especially important in today's mobile-first world, where users are spread across diverse devices, each with their own set of requirements and capabilities.

Benefits and Challenges of Developing for Multiple Platforms

Benefits:

1. **Cost and Time Efficiency:** By reusing the same codebase across multiple platforms, developers can significantly reduce development costs and the time it takes to bring the app to market. Rather than maintaining separate codebases for each platform, developers can focus on writing once and deploying everywhere.

2. **Consistent User Experience:** Cross-platform frameworks aim to provide a consistent user experience across platforms, which ensures that users have similar interactions and interfaces regardless of the device or OS they use.

3. **Broader Market Reach:** Developing cross-platform apps allows you to target a wider audience since your application can run on both mobile devices and desktop computers. This increases the app's reach and potential revenue.

4. **Faster Updates and Maintenance:** Since there is only one codebase to maintain, updates and bug fixes can be implemented more quickly and uniformly

across all platforms, reducing the overhead of dealing with platform-specific issues.

Challenges:

1. **Performance Issues:** Cross-platform frameworks can sometimes be slower than native apps because they add an additional layer between the application and the platform. This can lead to performance bottlenecks, especially for resource-intensive apps like games or real-time data applications.

2. **Platform-Specific Customization:** Even though you aim for a consistent experience, sometimes platform-specific adjustments are necessary to make the app feel native to each OS. These tweaks might require additional effort in terms of design, testing, and maintenance.

3. **Limited Access to Platform-Specific Features:** Cross-platform tools often do not provide the same level of access to platform-specific features that native development does. This can restrict the app's ability to leverage advanced functionalities offered by a particular platform, like custom animations or hardware features.

4. **Compatibility and Testing:** Ensuring the app functions correctly on all platforms can be challenging. Even with a shared codebase, there are still differences between platforms that might lead to unexpected issues. Comprehensive testing is essential to identify bugs that may not be immediately obvious on all platforms.

Overview of Python and C# in Cross-Platform Development

Python: Python is a highly versatile and user-friendly programming language. While it's traditionally seen as a backend development language, Python has found its place in cross-platform app development as well. Frameworks like **Kivy** and **BeeWare** allow developers to build cross-platform applications with Python that can run on desktop and mobile devices.

- **Kivy:** A popular open-source Python framework for building cross-platform applications. It supports Windows, macOS, Linux, Android, and iOS, and is especially useful for building touch-based applications.

- **BeeWare:** Another Python framework for building native user interfaces. BeeWare lets you develop apps that run on multiple platforms, including desktop and mobile, while preserving the look and feel of native applications.

15

C#: C# is a powerful, statically-typed language developed by Microsoft. It's primarily used in desktop and web applications, but with frameworks like **Xamarin** and **MAUI**, it has become a solid choice for cross-platform development.

- **Xamarin:** A popular C# framework for developing cross-platform apps for iOS, Android, and Windows using a shared C# codebase. Xamarin provides native performance and access to platform-specific APIs.
- **MAUI (Multi-platform App UI):** A more recent and advanced framework that is the evolution of Xamarin. It allows developers to build applications for Windows, macOS, iOS, and Android with a single shared codebase while offering a unified approach to UI and platform-specific features.

Both Python and C# are powerful languages in the cross-platform space, each with its own strengths and suitable use cases. Python's simplicity and extensive libraries make it ideal for rapid prototyping, while C# with its robust frameworks (Xamarin, MAUI) is a go-to for more complex and performance-sensitive apps.

Real-World Examples of Cross-Platform Applications

1. **Spotify:** The popular music streaming app uses cross-platform development techniques to ensure its availability on a wide range of devices. It's available on mobile, desktop, and even some gaming consoles, all while maintaining a consistent experience across platforms.

2. **WhatsApp:** WhatsApp, a widely-used messaging app, is available on multiple platforms including Android, iOS, and the web. The app uses a cross-platform approach, combining a native mobile experience with web-based integration.

3. **Slack:** Slack is a popular communication platform for teams. The app uses cross-platform technologies to ensure it works on desktop (Windows, macOS) and mobile (Android, iOS), helping users stay connected regardless of the device.

4. **Microsoft Teams:** Teams, part of Microsoft's suite of productivity tools, also uses cross-platform technologies to provide a seamless experience across Windows, macOS, iOS, and Android devices. This approach ensures businesses can rely on a single collaboration tool across diverse teams and devices.

This chapter provides an overview of cross-platform development, explaining why it's important, the pros and cons of developing for multiple platforms, and how Python and C# fit into the cross-platform landscape. By leveraging real-world examples, readers can see how large companies use cross-platform technologies to serve a global user base.

CHAPTER 2

FUNDAMENTALS OF PYTHON AND C# FOR CROSS-PLATFORM APPS

Basic Syntax and Structure of Python and C#

Python:

Python is known for its simplicity and readability, making it an excellent choice for beginners and experienced developers alike. Here's a basic overview of its syntax and structure:

- **Variables:** Python doesn't require explicit data types for variables. You can assign a value directly to a variable, and Python automatically infers the type.

  ```python
  name = "Alice"
  age = 30
  ```

- **Functions:** Functions are defined using the `def` keyword, followed by the function name and parameters in parentheses.

python

```python
def greet(name):
    print(f"Hello, {name}!")

greet("Alice")
```

- **Conditionals:** Python uses `if`, `elif`, and `else` to handle conditions.

python

```python
if age > 18:
    print("Adult")
else:
    print("Minor")
```

- **Loops:** Python provides `for` and `while` loops for iteration.

python

```python
for i in range(5):
    print(i)
```

- **Indentation:** Python uses indentation (typically 4 spaces) to define blocks of code, making the code visually clear.

C#:

C# is a statically-typed, object-oriented language developed by Microsoft. It follows a more formal structure and is designed for performance and scalability. Here's an overview of C# syntax:

- **Variables:** In C#, you must explicitly declare the data type of a variable.

```csharp
string name = "Alice";
int age = 30;
```

- **Functions:** Functions in C# are defined within classes using the `void` keyword for functions that don't return a value.

```csharp
void Greet(string name)
{
    Console.WriteLine($"Hello, {name}!");
```

21

```
}
```

```
Greet("Alice");
```

- **Conditionals:** C# uses `if`, `else  if`, and `else` for condition handling.

```
csharp
```

```
if (age > 18)
    Console.WriteLine("Adult");
else
    Console.WriteLine("Minor");
```

- **Loops:** C# offers a variety of looping structures, including `for`, `while`, and `foreach`.

```
csharp
```

```
for (int i = 0; i < 5; i++)
{
    Console.WriteLine(i);
}
```

- **Braces:** Unlike Python, C# uses curly braces `{}` to define blocks of code.

Key Differences and Similarities Between Python and C#

Similarities:

1. **Both are High-Level Languages:** Both Python and C# are high-level programming languages, which means they abstract away most of the complex operations like memory management, making them easier to use.

2. **Both Support Object-Oriented Programming (OOP):** Python and C# both support OOP principles like classes, objects, inheritance, and polymorphism. This allows developers to organize and structure code more efficiently.

3. **Both Have Extensive Libraries and Frameworks:** Python and C# both come with rich libraries and frameworks to speed up development. For example, Python has libraries like Flask and Django for web development, while C# has .NET Core and Xamarin for building cross-platform apps.

Differences:

1. **Typing System:**

o **Python:** Python is dynamically typed, meaning variable types are determined at runtime. This provides flexibility but can lead to runtime errors.

o **C#:** C# is statically typed, meaning you must declare the type of variables. This can lead to fewer bugs and better performance but requires more upfront work.

Example:

o **Python:**

```python
x = 10  # No need to declare type
```

o **C#:**

```csharp
int x = 10;  // Must declare type
```

2. **Syntax and Structure:**

o **Python:** Python's syntax is simple and minimalistic. It uses indentation to define blocks of code, making the code more readable but also more sensitive to formatting errors.

- C#: C# uses braces { } to define blocks of code, which might be more familiar to developers coming from languages like Java or C++.

3. **Platform and Ecosystem:**

   - **Python:** Python is cross-platform and can run on almost any operating system. However, it's not typically used for mobile app development unless using frameworks like Kivy or BeeWare.

   - **C#:** C# is traditionally associated with Windows but, with the introduction of .NET Core and Xamarin, it now supports cross-platform development for macOS, Linux, Android, and iOS.

4. **Performance:**

   - **Python:** Python tends to be slower than C# due to its dynamic nature and interpreted execution.

   - **C#:** C# is compiled to intermediate code, which is then executed by the Common Language Runtime (CLR), making it faster and more efficient, especially for larger and more performance-sensitive applications.

5. **Memory Management:**

   - **Python:** Python uses automatic memory management and garbage collection, which makes it easier to use but can lead to less control over memory.

- o **C#:** C# also uses garbage collection but offers more control over memory management, particularly in scenarios that require performance optimization.

How to Choose the Right Language for Your Project

When deciding between Python and C# for cross-platform app development, several factors should guide your decision:

1. **Project Complexity:**
   - o For simple to moderately complex apps, Python is often a great choice due to its ease of use and fast development cycle.
   - o If your app requires high performance, more control over resources, or if you're developing a large-scale enterprise application, C# may be a better choice due to its strong typing, robust performance, and scalability.

2. **Platform Support:**
   - o **Python** is ideal for web, desktop, and server-side applications. If you're focused on creating web apps or backend services, Python with frameworks like Django or Flask is a solid option.
   - o **C#** shines for mobile development (using Xamarin or MAUI), desktop applications (via

.NET Core or WPF), and cloud-based enterprise solutions (Azure).

3. **Development Speed:**

   o **Python** is great for rapid prototyping, proof-of-concept development, and startups that need to get an app to market quickly. The language's simple syntax and large number of libraries allow for faster development.

   o **C#** might take longer to develop in the early stages due to its more verbose nature, but its performance benefits and strong type system can result in more maintainable and scalable code in the long run.

4. **Community and Ecosystem:**

   o **Python** has a huge community and a wide array of libraries, particularly for data science, machine learning, and web development.

   o **C#** has a well-established ecosystem, particularly for desktop applications, cloud services, and games, with robust support in enterprise-level environments.

In Summary, **Python** is great for quick development cycles and projects requiring simplicity and flexibility, while **C#** is suited for more complex, performance-oriented applications, especially when building for multiple platforms like mobile or desktop with advanced functionality.

This chapter provides a foundation for understanding Python and C# in cross-platform development. It outlines the basics of their syntax and structure, highlights their key differences and similarities, and helps you decide which language is better suited for your project based on your specific needs and goals.

CHAPTER 3

UNDERSTANDING MODERN FRAMEWORKS

Introduction to Popular Frameworks

In the world of software development, frameworks play a crucial role in helping developers build robust, scalable, and maintainable applications efficiently. Frameworks provide a set of pre-built tools and libraries that simplify the development process, allowing developers to focus on the unique aspects of their application rather than reinventing the wheel. Here are some of the most popular frameworks for cross-platform development:

1. **.NET Core** (C#):
    o   **Overview:** .NET Core is a cross-platform framework developed by Microsoft for building web applications, desktop applications, microservices, and more. It's a modern, open-source version of the traditional .NET Framework, designed to work across Windows, macOS, and Linux.

o **Key Features:** Performance optimization, scalability, support for RESTful APIs, and seamless integration with cloud services like Microsoft Azure. .NET Core allows developers to create both client-side and server-side applications with a unified development model.

2. **Flask** (Python):

o **Overview:** Flask is a lightweight and flexible web framework for Python. It's a microframework, meaning it provides the essentials for building web apps but leaves developers with the freedom to choose additional libraries or tools as needed.

o **Key Features:** Flask is known for its simplicity and minimalism. It doesn't come with built-in database support, form validation, or other features you might find in a larger framework like Django, making it more suited for smaller, simpler projects or applications that require customization.

3. **Django** (Python):

o **Overview:** Django is a high-level Python framework designed to encourage rapid development and clean, pragmatic design. It comes with everything you need to build a web app right out of the box, including an ORM

(Object-Relational Mapper), authentication, URL routing, and more.

- o **Key Features:** Django emphasizes "don't repeat yourself" (DRY), which encourages developers to reuse code and reduce redundancy. It includes an admin interface for managing application data, making it ideal for projects requiring a content management system (CMS).

4. **React Native** (JavaScript):

- o **Overview:** React Native is a framework developed by Facebook for building mobile applications using JavaScript and React. With React Native, developers can write applications that run on both iOS and Android using a single codebase, which makes it one of the most popular tools for cross-platform mobile development.

- o **Key Features:** React Native uses native components, which allows apps to have performance close to that of native apps while being easier to develop due to the shared codebase. It also integrates well with other native modules and third-party libraries, making it highly versatile.

The Role of Frameworks in Simplifying Cross-Platform Development

Modern frameworks are instrumental in simplifying cross-platform development. They offer a range of benefits that allow developers to create applications that work seamlessly across different operating systems and devices. Here's how frameworks help streamline the development process:

1. **Code Reusability:** Frameworks provide reusable components, modules, and libraries, which means developers don't have to start from scratch for each new project. For example, with frameworks like React Native or Django, much of the basic functionality (authentication, routing, UI components) is already built in, saving development time.

2. **Cross-Platform Compatibility:** Many modern frameworks, like .NET Core and React Native, are designed specifically to support multiple platforms. This means developers can write the code once and deploy it across different devices and operating systems (iOS, Android, Windows, Linux, macOS). This is especially important for businesses looking to

reach a broad audience without the high cost of developing separate applications for each platform.

3. **Faster Development Cycle:** By providing pre-built tools, templates, and libraries, frameworks allow developers to build applications faster. For example, Django's admin interface makes it easy to manage the content of a web application, while Flask's minimalistic approach gives developers more control over the customization of the app.

4. **Improved Performance:** Many frameworks, particularly those focused on mobile app development, offer optimizations that improve performance across different platforms. React Native's use of native components helps apps run more smoothly on mobile devices, and .NET Core's performance improvements help web applications handle large amounts of traffic.

5. **Security:** Frameworks often come with built-in security features, such as secure authentication mechanisms and protection against common vulnerabilities like SQL injection and cross-site scripting (XSS). Django, for example, has a built-in authentication system that makes securing user accounts easier. This allows developers to focus on

building the core features of their apps, rather than worrying about security.

6. **Scalability:** As applications grow in complexity and user demand, scalability becomes critical. Modern frameworks like .NET Core and Django are designed to scale efficiently, making it easier to handle a large number of users or data without performance issues.

Real-World Case Studies of Apps Built with These Frameworks

1. **.NET Core:**

   o **Stack Overflow:** The popular question-and-answer website uses .NET Core for both its backend and API services. The platform supports millions of users, and its developers chose .NET Core for its performance and scalability, which allowed the platform to handle increasing traffic while maintaining fast response times.

   o **Microsoft Teams:** Microsoft Teams is a collaboration platform built on .NET Core. The app supports messaging, video calls, file sharing, and much more. It is designed to work seamlessly across Windows, macOS, iOS, and Android, and .NET Core was a key part of making the app cross-platform while maintaining high performance.

2. **Flask:**

   o **Airbnb:** Airbnb, the popular home-sharing platform, uses Flask for its backend to manage some of its core web functionality. Flask's lightweight nature made it ideal for Airbnb's needs, allowing them to create a custom backend while integrating with other tools and services.

   o **Netflix:** While Netflix's entire tech stack is large and diverse, parts of it leverage Flask for handling microservices, particularly in regions where simplicity and scalability are paramount.

3. **Django:**

   o **Instagram:** Instagram, the popular social media platform, was initially built using Django. The framework allowed Instagram to rapidly develop new features and handle its massive user base, including everything from photo uploads to direct messaging. Django's built-in admin interface and ORM made it easy to manage data, while its scalability ensured Instagram could grow without compromising performance.

   o **Pinterest:** Pinterest also uses Django for various parts of its web platform. The framework's ability to handle high-traffic applications, along with its robust security features, made it a good fit for

Pinterest as the platform scaled to millions of users.

4. **React Native:**

   o **Facebook:** As the framework's creator, Facebook uses React Native for its mobile app to maintain cross-platform compatibility with iOS and Android. React Native allows Facebook to keep the same user interface across platforms while ensuring smooth performance and easy updates.

   o **Uber:** Uber uses React Native for parts of its driver and rider apps. React Native allows Uber to manage features like ride requests, driver location tracking, and payments across both iOS and Android platforms without needing separate codebases.

   o **Skype:** Skype's mobile app was built with React Native to streamline development and improve performance. By using a shared codebase for both iOS and Android, Skype reduced development time while maintaining the functionality needed for video calling, messaging, and file sharing.

This chapter provided a detailed look at some of the most popular frameworks used for cross-platform development today. By understanding the role of frameworks like .NET Core, Flask, Django, and React Native, you can see how they simplify and accelerate the development process. Additionally, the case studies highlight how these frameworks have been used to create real-world applications that serve millions of users across various platforms.

CHAPTER 4

SETTING UP YOUR DEVELOPMENT ENVIRONMENT

Setting up the right development environment is essential for any software project. It ensures smooth workflows, efficient coding, and easy management of dependencies. This chapter covers how to set up your environment for Python and C# development, including necessary tools and best practices for handling dependencies.

Installing Python, C#, and Necessary Tools (IDEs, Package Managers)

1. **Installing Python:**
   - **Download Python:** Visit the official Python website at python.org and download the latest version compatible with your operating system (Windows, macOS, or Linux).
   - **Installation on Windows:**
     - After downloading the installer, run it and make sure to check the box that says "Add Python to PATH" before proceeding with the installation.

38

- o **Installation on macOS/Linux:**

  - On macOS, Python can be installed via Homebrew by running the command:

    ```bash
    brew install python
    ```

  - On Linux, Python is usually pre-installed. If not, you can install it via a package manager:

    ```bash
    sudo apt-get install python3
    ```

2. **Installing C#:**

   - o **Download Visual Studio:** To start developing with C#, download Visual Studio, a popular Integrated Development Environment (IDE) for C# development. You can download it from the Visual Studio website.

     - For cross-platform development with .NET Core, the free version **Visual Studio Code** (VS Code) is a lightweight alternative and can be paired with the .NET SDK for C# development.

   - o **Installation on Windows:**

39

- Download and run the Visual Studio installer. During the installation process, select the ".NET desktop development" workload to install the necessary tools for C# development.
  o **Installation on macOS/Linux:**
    - On macOS, you can install Visual Studio Code from the official website and then install the C# extension.
    - On Linux, you can install Visual Studio Code via the terminal:

    ```bash

    sudo snap install --classic code
    ```

3. **Installing Package Managers:**
   o **Python:** Use **pip**, Python's package manager, to install libraries and dependencies.
     - To check if pip is installed, run:

     ```bash

     pip --version
     ```

     - To install packages, use:

```
bash

pip install <package-name>
```

- o **C#: NuGet** is the package manager for C#. Visual Studio automatically installs NuGet when you set up your development environment. You can use it directly within Visual Studio or through the command line via the .NET CLI.
    - To install a package with NuGet:

```
bash

dotnet add package <package-
name>
```

Working with Virtual Environments in Python and Managing Dependencies

Virtual environments allow developers to isolate project-specific dependencies and avoid conflicts between different versions of libraries. This is particularly important in Python, where multiple projects may require different versions of the same library.

1. **Creating a Virtual Environment in Python:**
    - o Open a terminal or command prompt and navigate to your project directory.

41

o   To create a virtual environment, use the following command:

```bash

python -m venv myenv
```

o   **Activating the Virtual Environment:**
- On Windows:

```bash

myenv\Scripts\activate
```

- On macOS/Linux:

```bash

source myenv/bin/activate
```

o   **Installing Dependencies in the Virtual Environment:**
- Once activated, you can install dependencies using `pip` without affecting the global Python environment:

```bash

pip install <package-name>
```

o **Deactivating the Virtual Environment:**

  ▪ When you're done, you can deactivate the virtual environment by running:

```bash
```

```
deactivate
```

2. Managing Dependencies:

o To make it easier to replicate the environment for other developers or on different machines, create a **requirements.txt** file that lists all of your dependencies:

```bash
```

```
pip freeze > requirements.txt
```

o You can then install all dependencies in the requirements file with:

```bash
```

```
pip install -r requirements.txt
```

Setting Up .NET Core for C# Development

To develop cross-platform applications using C# and .NET Core, you need to install the .NET SDK, which includes everything you need to build, test, and run .NET applications.

1. **Installing .NET Core:**

   o **Download .NET SDK:** Visit the official .NET website at dotnet.microsoft.com and download the latest version of the .NET SDK compatible with your operating system.

   o **Installation on Windows:**

      ▪ Run the installer after downloading, and follow the installation prompts.

   o **Installation on macOS/Linux:**

      ▪ On macOS, you can install the .NET SDK via Homebrew:

      ```bash
      brew install --cask dotnet-sdk
      ```

      ▪ On Linux, you can use the following command:

      ```bash
      sudo apt-get install dotnet-sdk-<version>
      ```

2. **Creating a .NET Core Project:**

o   To create a new .NET Core project, run the following command:

```bash
```

```
dotnet new console -n MyProject
```

o   This creates a new console application named **MyProject** in your current directory.

o   **Running the Project:**

- Navigate to the project folder and run the application:

```bash
```

```
cd MyProject
dotnet run
```

Real-World Examples of How to Streamline Your Development Environment

1. **Using Docker for Cross-Platform Development:** Docker allows you to containerize your applications and ensure they run consistently across different environments. By using Docker, you can package your Python or C# app along with all its dependencies and run it in any environment, regardless of the host system.

o For Python, you can create a Dockerfile to define the environment and dependencies for your application. This ensures that the app will behave the same on every machine.

o For C#, you can use a Dockerfile with .NET Core to create a containerized .NET application that can be easily deployed across different platforms.

2. **Integrating Version Control with Git:** Set up **Git** for version control to manage your codebase and collaborate with others. By using Git with GitHub, GitLab, or Bitbucket, you can track changes, manage multiple branches, and easily share your code with other developers. Integrating Git into your workflow ensures that your development process is streamlined and organized.

3. **Using IDE Extensions and Plugins:** Both Visual Studio and Visual Studio Code (VS Code) offer a wide variety of extensions and plugins that enhance your development environment. For Python, you can install extensions like **Python** for VS Code, which provides features like IntelliSense, linting, and debugging support. For C#, the **C# for Visual Studio Code** extension provides syntax highlighting, debugging, and other tools to make C# development smoother in VS Code.

4. **Setting Up Continuous Integration (CI) and Continuous Deployment (CD):** Streamline your workflow with CI/CD pipelines using tools like **GitHub Actions**, **Azure DevOps**, or **Jenkins**. These tools automate the process of building, testing, and deploying your applications. By setting up CI/CD pipelines, you can ensure that your code is tested and deployed consistently across different platforms and environments.

This chapter has guided you through setting up your development environment for both Python and C# development, highlighting essential tools like IDEs, package managers, and virtual environments. We also discussed how to streamline your workflow by using Docker, version control, and CI/CD tools. A well-configured development environment is the foundation of efficient cross-platform development, allowing you to work seamlessly across different platforms and devices.

CHAPTER 5

BUILDING YOUR FIRST CROSS-PLATFORM APP

In this chapter, we will walk through the process of building a simple to-do list application using both **Python** and **C#**. The purpose of this exercise is to introduce you to core programming concepts such as functions, loops, and conditionals, while demonstrating how to create a functional, cross-platform app in both languages.

We'll break down the steps clearly and ensure that you gain hands-on experience by building the app from scratch. Let's get started!

Step-by-Step Guide to Building a Simple App in Python and C#

Python (Using Flask for Web App Development)

We'll use **Flask**, a simple web framework, to create the to-do list app in Python. This will give us the ability to run the app in any browser, making it cross-platform compatible.

1. Setting Up the Environment:

- ○ Install Flask via **pip** (Python's package manager).

```bash
```

```bash
pip install flask
```

- ○ Create a new directory for your project and navigate to it:

```bash
```

```bash
mkdir todo-flask-app
cd todo-flask-app
```

2. Create the Main App File:

- ○ Create a file named `app.py` in your project directory. This will be the main Python file that runs the Flask app.
- ○ Inside `app.py`, write the following code to set up Flask and create a basic route:

```python
```

```python
from flask import Flask, render_template,
request, redirect

app = Flask(__name__)
```

```
todos = []

@app.route('/')
def home():
    return  render_template('index.html',
todos=todos)

@app.route('/add', methods=['POST'])
def add_todo():
    todo = request.form['todo']
    todos.append(todo)
    return redirect('/')

@app.route('/delete/<int:index>')
def delete_todo(index):
    todos.pop(index)
    return redirect('/')

if __name__ == "__main__":
    app.run(debug=True)
```

3. **Creating the Front-End (HTML):**

   o In the same project directory, create a folder called `templates`. Inside the `templates` folder, create a file called `index.html`.

   o The `index.html` file will render the to-do list and provide a simple form to add new tasks:

```
html
```

```
<!DOCTYPE html>
<html lang="en">
<head>
    <meta charset="UTF-8">
    <meta                 name="viewport"
content="width=device-width,        initial-
scale=1.0">
    <title>To-Do List</title>
</head>
<body>
    <h1>To-Do List</h1>
    <ul>
        {% for todo in todos %}
            <li>{{       todo      }}      <a
href="/delete/{{           loop.index0
}}">Delete</a></li>
        {% endfor %}
    </ul>
    <form action="/add" method="POST">
        <input   type="text"   name="todo"
placeholder="New task" required>
        <button type="submit">Add</button>
    </form>
</body>
</html>
```

4. Running the Flask App:

    o   In the terminal, run your Flask app:

```
bash

python app.py
```

- o Open a browser and navigate to http://127.0.0.1:5000/. You should see a simple to-do list app where you can add and remove tasks.

C# (Using .NET Core for a Console App)

In C#, we will create a console application to build the to-do list app. This will run in the terminal, making it cross-platform compatible on Windows, macOS, and Linux.

1. **Setting Up the Environment:**
   - o First, make sure you have **.NET Core SDK** installed. You can download it from dotnet.microsoft.com.
   - o Create a new console application by running:

```
bash

dotnet new console -n TodoApp
cd TodoApp
```

2. Create the Main App Logic:

o Open the `Program.cs` file. This file contains the main program logic, where you will define the to-do list functionality.

```csharp
using System;
using System.Collections.Generic;

class Program
{
    static List<string> todos = new List<string>();

    static void Main(string[] args)
    {
        while (true)
        {
            Console.Clear();
            Console.WriteLine("To-Do List");
            Console.WriteLine("----------");
            ShowTodos();
            Console.WriteLine("\nChoose an option:");
            Console.WriteLine("1.    Add task");
```

```
            Console.WriteLine("2.    Remove
task");

            Console.WriteLine("3. Exit");

            string        choice        =
Console.ReadLine();

            if (choice == "1")
            {
                AddTask();
            }
            else if (choice == "2")
            {
                RemoveTask();
            }
            else if (choice == "3")
            {
                break;
            }
            else
            {

Console.WriteLine("Invalid choice! Please
try again.");
            }
        }
    }


    static void ShowTodos()
```

```
    {
        if (todos.Count == 0)
        {
            Console.WriteLine("No tasks in
your to-do list.");
        }
        else
        {
            for  (int  i  =  0;  i  <
todos.Count; i++)
            {
                Console.WriteLine($"{i  +
1}. {todos[i]}");
            }
        }
    }

    static void AddTask()
    {
        Console.Write("Enter new task: ");
        string task = Console.ReadLine();
        todos.Add(task);
    }

    static void RemoveTask()
    {
        Console.Write("Enter  task  number
to remove: ");
```

```
        if
(int.TryParse(Console.ReadLine(),  out  int
taskNumber) && taskNumber > 0 && taskNumber
<= todos.Count)
        {
            todos.RemoveAt(taskNumber    -
1);
        }
        else
        {
            Console.WriteLine("Invalid
task number.");
        }
    }
}
```

3. **Running the C# Console App:**

   o   Build and run the application by executing the following command:

   ```
   bash
   ```

   ```
   dotnet run
   ```

   o   The app will run in the terminal, and you can interact with it by adding and removing tasks from the list.

Introduction to Core Programming Concepts

1. **Functions:** Functions are blocks of reusable code that perform a specific task. In both Python and C#, we used functions to define the behavior of our app. For instance, `add_todo()` in Python and `AddTask()` in C# are functions that add new tasks to the to-do list.

2. **Loops:** Loops allow us to repeat a block of code multiple times. In the Python Flask app, we used a loop to display all the to-do items in `index.html`. Similarly, in the C# console app, we used a `while` loop to continually prompt the user for input until they choose to exit.

3. **Conditionals:** Conditional statements like `if`, `elif`, and `else` (Python) or `if` and `else` (C#) are used to make decisions in your code. These are vital for controlling the flow of the app. For example, in the C# app, we used conditionals to check if the user chose to add or remove a task.

Hands-On Project: A Basic To-Do List App

Through the step-by-step guide, you've now created a simple to-do list app in both Python and C#. Here's a quick recap of the features implemented:

- **Add Tasks:** Users can add tasks to the list.
- **Delete Tasks:** Users can remove tasks by selecting the task number (C#) or clicking a "Delete" link (Python).
- **Cross-Platform:** Both apps work across multiple platforms. The Python app runs in a browser, and the C# app runs in the terminal.

This hands-on project has introduced core programming concepts like functions, loops, and conditionals, as well as practical experience with both Python and C# for building cross-platform applications.

In the next chapters, we will continue expanding on these foundations and delve into more complex functionality as you develop larger, more powerful cross-platform applications.

CHAPTER 6

MOBILE CROSS-PLATFORM DEVELOPMENT WITH PYTHON AND C#

In this chapter, we will explore the world of mobile cross-platform development using **Python** and **C#**. Mobile apps today need to function seamlessly across multiple platforms—primarily iOS and Android—without the need to write separate code for each. Cross-platform development allows developers to build one app and deploy it to multiple platforms, saving time, resources, and effort.

We'll take a closer look at popular frameworks that allow you to achieve this and walk you through the process of building a mobile app using both Python and C#. We'll also provide real-world examples of successful mobile apps built with these technologies.

Overview of Mobile Frameworks: Kivy, Xamarin, and React Native

1. Kivy (Python)

- **What It Is:** Kivy is an open-source Python framework used for building cross-platform mobile applications. It's best suited for applications with rich, interactive user interfaces such as games, multimedia apps, and apps that require multi-touch support.

- **Key Features:**
  - Supports Windows, macOS, Linux, iOS, and Android.
  - Provides a wide range of UI controls and a customizable framework for touch-based input.
  - Ideal for building apps with a graphical or game-like interface.
  - Includes tools for building and packaging apps for mobile platforms.

- **When to Use:** Kivy is an excellent choice if you're already familiar with Python and need to create mobile applications that include complex UI components, such as games or apps that involve gesture-based control.

2. Xamarin (C#)

- **What It Is:** Xamarin is a Microsoft-owned framework that allows developers to create cross-platform apps using C# and .NET. It compiles C# code into native code, ensuring the app performs well on iOS and Android.

- **Key Features:**
  - o One codebase for iOS, Android, and Windows.
  - o Access to native APIs, making it possible to build apps that are indistinguishable from native apps.
  - o Xamarin.Forms allows developers to design UIs that work across platforms.
  - o Integration with Azure and cloud services for enterprise applications.
- **When to Use:** Xamarin is perfect for developers already familiar with C# and the .NET ecosystem who need to build enterprise-grade apps with high performance and access to native device features.

3. React Native (JavaScript)

- **What It Is:** React Native is a framework created by Facebook that allows developers to build mobile apps using JavaScript and React. It lets you write a single codebase and deploy it to both iOS and Android while still having the ability to call native components when necessary.
- **Key Features:**

- o Uses native components to ensure apps perform well and feel "native."
- o Large community support and a wide range of third-party libraries.
- o Allows code sharing between platforms and provides the ability to write platform-specific code.
- o Reusable components and live reloading for faster development cycles.

- **When to Use:** React Native is ideal for web developers familiar with React who want to extend their skills to mobile app development. It's also a great choice if you want to rapidly prototype or iterate on mobile apps, thanks to its performance and flexibility.

Building Mobile Apps Using Python and C#

Building a Mobile App with Python (Using Kivy)

1. Setting Up Your Environment:

- o Install Kivy by running:

```bash
bash
```

```
pip install kivy
```

2. Creating a Basic Mobile App:

o Let's build a simple app that displays a button. When clicked, the button changes text.

o **Code (Python with Kivy):**

```python
python

from kivy.app import App
from kivy.uix.button import Button

class MyApp(App):
    def build(self):
        button = Button(text="Click me")

        button.bind(on_press=self.change_text)
        return button

    def change_text(self, instance):
        instance.text = "You clicked me!"

if __name__ == "__main__":
    MyApp().run()
```

3. **Running the App:**

   o To run the app on Android or iOS, you would need to package the app using **Buildozer** (for Android) or **Xcode** (for iOS). Packaging instructions are available in the Kivy documentation, but for a quick test, the app can be run on desktop as well.

4. **Packaging for Mobile:**

   o To package for Android, use **Buildozer**:

   ```bash
   bash
   ```

   ```
   buildozer init      #  Initializes
   configuration
   buildozer android debug  # Builds the
   app for Android
   ```

Building a Mobile App with C# (Using Xamarin)

1. **Setting Up Your Environment:**

   o Install **Visual Studio** with the **Xamarin** workload. You can download Visual Studio from here.

2. **Creating a New Xamarin App:**

   o Open Visual Studio, create a new Xamarin.Forms project, and select "Blank App" for a mobile app that works on both Android and iOS.

3. Designing the UI:

o In the **MainPage.xaml** file, design a simple UI with a button and a label:

xml

```xml
<?xml version="1.0" encoding="utf-8"?>
<ContentPage
xmlns="http://xamarin.com/schemas/2014/forms"

xmlns:x="http://schemas.microsoft.com/winfx/2006/xaml"

x:Class="TodoApp.MainPage">

    <StackLayout>
        <Button    Text="Click    Me"
Clicked="OnButtonClicked" />
        <Label   x:Name="outputLabel"
Text="Hello, Xamarin!" />
    </StackLayout>
</ContentPage>
```

4. Adding Logic (C#):

o In the **MainPage.xaml.cs** file, add the logic for the button click event:

```csharp
using System;
using Xamarin.Forms;

namespace TodoApp
{
    public partial class MainPage :
ContentPage
    {
        public MainPage()
        {
            InitializeComponent();
        }

        private              void
OnButtonClicked(object       sender,
EventArgs e)
        {
            outputLabel.Text = "You
clicked the button!";
        }
    }
}
```

5. **Running the App:**
   o You can now run the app on an Android or iOS simulator directly from Visual Studio, or deploy it to a physical device for testing.

Real-World Examples of Mobile Apps and Their Cross-Platform Implementation

1. **Instagram (React Native):** Instagram, one of the most popular social media platforms, uses **React Native** for parts of its mobile application. By using React Native, Instagram was able to build and maintain a single codebase for both iOS and Android platforms, drastically reducing development time. The app's performance is near-native, and the development team benefits from the shared code between platforms.

2. **WhatsApp (Xamarin):** WhatsApp, the popular messaging app, uses **Xamarin** to create cross-platform mobile applications for iOS, Android, and Windows. The use of Xamarin allows WhatsApp to maintain a native user interface and leverage platform-specific APIs, while still using a shared codebase for faster updates and bug fixes.

3. **Spotify (Kivy/Python):** While Spotify's mobile app isn't entirely built with Python, the company uses **Kivy** for some internal tools and apps, particularly for data visualization and dashboard management. This showcases how Python, via frameworks like

Kivy, can be used for mobile development, especially for more specific use cases like analytics or internal tools.

4. **Airbnb (React Native):** Airbnb transitioned to **React Native** to streamline its mobile app development. By using React Native, Airbnb was able to share 90% of the codebase between iOS and Android, improving both development speed and app performance. React Native allows Airbnb to focus on delivering a smooth user experience without worrying about platform-specific code too much.

Summary

Mobile cross-platform development is an efficient and practical way to build apps that run seamlessly across multiple platforms. In this chapter, we introduced you to the most popular mobile frameworks—**Kivy** for Python, **Xamarin** for C#, and **React Native** for JavaScript. We also provided hands-on examples of building simple mobile apps using both Python and C#.

By understanding and utilizing these frameworks, you can create powerful mobile apps that run on Android, iOS, and even other platforms, all while writing less code and maximizing efficiency. Whether you choose Python, C#, or another framework, the key is understanding the trade-offs and selecting the right tool for your project's needs.

CHAPTER 7

DESIGNING USER INTERFACES FOR CROSS-PLATFORM APPS

User Interface (UI) and User Experience (UX) are at the heart of any successful application. Whether you're developing for web, mobile, or desktop, creating an intuitive and visually appealing interface is critical. In this chapter, we'll discuss the key principles of UI/UX design, introduce popular cross-platform UI frameworks, explore best practices for designing intuitive UIs, and analyze case studies of cross-platform apps that excel in UI/UX.

Principles of UI/UX Design

UI Design focuses on the look and feel of an application— its layout, colors, fonts, and interactive elements. **UX Design**, on the other hand, focuses on the overall experience of the user, ensuring the app is easy to use and that it fulfills the needs of the user efficiently.

Here are the key principles that guide both UI and UX design:

1. **Clarity**:
   - The interface should be clear and easy to navigate. Avoid unnecessary elements and clutter that could distract or confuse users. Prioritize content that is important and relevant.
   - Use readable fonts, clear labels for buttons, and straightforward icons that users can easily understand at a glance.

2. **Consistency**:
   - Consistent design elements help users become familiar with the app quickly. Maintain a uniform color palette, typography, and layout throughout the app.
   - Use consistent iconography and terminology, and follow established design patterns to reduce the learning curve.

3. **User-Centered Design**:
   - Always consider the user's needs and goals. The app should solve a problem for the user and be designed to make their tasks as easy as possible.
   - Gather feedback from real users and iterate on your designs. This might include usability testing, A/B testing, or surveys.

4. **Feedback and Responsiveness**:

   o Users should know what's happening within the app. If an action is taking place, such as a button being clicked or a form being submitted, provide feedback. This can be done with visual cues (e.g., a loading spinner) or through sound and haptic feedback.

   o Interactive elements should respond instantly to user input, which improves the user experience by making it feel intuitive and fluid.

5. **Simplicity**:

   o Keep the interface simple. Avoid overwhelming users with too much information or too many choices. Stick to the essentials and provide the user with only what they need at that moment.

   o Use clear navigation flows and avoid unnecessary steps in achieving tasks.

6. **Accessibility**:

   o Design for all users, including those with disabilities. Make sure your app is usable with screen readers, and offer adjustable font sizes, high-contrast themes, and other features to accommodate a range of needs.

Cross-Platform UI Frameworks: React Native, Xamarin.Forms, Kivy

Let's explore the popular cross-platform UI frameworks that help you design and develop intuitive user interfaces for mobile and desktop applications:

1. React Native:

- **Overview:** React Native is a JavaScript framework created by Facebook that allows developers to build mobile applications using the same design principles as React for the web. React Native uses native components, providing high performance and smooth user interfaces across iOS and Android devices.

- **UI Design:** React Native allows you to design UIs using a declarative syntax that makes your code easy to understand. Components like `View`, `Text`, `Button`, and `Image` are rendered to native views on both platforms, ensuring a seamless experience.

- **Customization:** React Native allows you to use custom native components when needed, and it integrates well with third-party libraries like **React Navigation** and **NativeBase** to enhance UI design.

2. Xamarin.Forms:

- **Overview:** Xamarin.Forms is part of the Xamarin framework and allows developers to create cross-platform apps with a single codebase. Xamarin.Forms provides a way to design UIs that automatically adjust to the specific platform (iOS, Android, and UWP) while maintaining a consistent look and feel.

- **UI Design:** Xamarin.Forms uses a shared UI definition, where the UI is written in XAML (eXtensible Application Markup Language). It supports data binding, control templates, and animations to build rich, interactive UIs.

- **Customization:** While Xamarin.Forms provides a set of built-in controls, it also allows for native controls when needed, making it highly customizable and flexible.

3. Kivy:

- **Overview:** Kivy is a Python-based framework for building cross-platform applications that run on Windows, macOS, Linux, Android, and iOS. Kivy is particularly useful for developing apps with complex graphical user interfaces, such as games or interactive apps.

- **UI Design:** Kivy provides a wide range of built-in widgets (buttons, sliders, labels) and layouts (boxes, grids, stack layouts) that make it easy to design interactive UIs. The framework also supports gestures and multi-touch input, which is essential for mobile app development.

- **Customization:** Kivy is highly customizable, allowing you to design your UI exactly how you want it. It uses **Kv Language**, a domain-specific language that separates design from logic, making UI design more straightforward.

Best Practices for Creating Intuitive User Interfaces

Designing a successful, intuitive UI is crucial for providing a great user experience. Here are some best practices to help you build effective cross-platform UIs:

1. **Design for Touch and Gesture:**
   - Mobile apps require special attention to touch interactions. Ensure that interactive elements (buttons, sliders, etc.) are large enough to be easily tapped, and support common gestures like swiping, pinching, and scrolling.
   - **React Native** and **Kivy** both provide built-in support for handling touch gestures, so you can easily implement features like pinch-to-zoom or swipe navigation.

2. **Prioritize Key Actions:**

o Make it easy for users to perform the most important tasks. Whether it's making a purchase, sending a message, or viewing content, the most critical actions should be front and center in your design.

o Use clear, concise labels for buttons and ensure that users can easily navigate to their most common tasks.

3. **Minimize Clutter:**

o Keep the UI clean and free of unnecessary elements. Display only the most essential content, and provide clear visual hierarchies to guide the user's attention.

o In **React Native** and **Xamarin.Forms**, make use of collapsible menus, tabs, or accordions to keep your UI neat and organized.

4. **Use Familiar UI Patterns:**

o Stick to common user interface patterns and conventions so that users feel comfortable interacting with your app. For example, use a **tab bar** for navigation, provide a **hamburger menu** for options, and ensure that buttons and icons are intuitive.

o Many UI frameworks like **Xamarin.Forms** provide pre-built controls that follow these established patterns, reducing the amount of custom design you need to do.

5. **Ensure Consistent Feedback:**

   o Provide users with clear, immediate feedback for their actions. When a button is clicked, show a visual change (e.g., button press animation, loading spinner). This helps users feel confident that their actions are being processed.

   o **React Native** and **Kivy** support feedback mechanisms like animations, visual changes, and even sounds to confirm actions.

6. **Test Across Devices:**

   o Your app will be used across a variety of devices with different screen sizes, resolutions, and aspect ratios. Always test your UI on different devices to ensure it looks good and functions well across all platforms.

   o Use **Xamarin.Forms** or **Kivy** to design responsive layouts that adapt to different screen sizes, or use **React Native's** responsive design tools like `flexbox`.

Case Studies of Cross-Platform Apps with Great UI/UX

1. **Instagram (React Native):** Instagram is one of the best-known apps built with **React Native**, and its clean, visually engaging UI has played a large part in its success. The app's navigation, image feed, and direct messaging UI all feel native, and users have a seamless experience when switching between iOS and Android devices. Instagram's use of animations, fast performance, and smooth transitions exemplifies excellent UI/UX design in a cross-platform environment.

2. **Uber (Xamarin.Forms):** Uber's mobile app, built with **Xamarin.Forms**, provides a consistent experience on iOS and Android, despite the differences in the underlying platforms. The app uses familiar UI patterns, such as a map interface and large, tappable buttons for requesting rides. The seamless integration of maps and real-time updates ensures users always know where their ride is, making for a smooth and intuitive UX.

3. **Khan Academy (Kivy/Python):** The educational platform **Khan Academy** leverages **Kivy** to create cross-platform applications with engaging, interactive user interfaces. The app features a simple

design that's easy to navigate, with easy-to-read text, colorful graphics, and interactive learning modules that make education more fun and intuitive. Kivy's ability to create dynamic, touch-friendly UIs is key to its success.

Summary

UI/UX design plays a pivotal role in the success of cross-platform apps. Whether you're using **React Native**, **Xamarin.Forms**, or **Kivy**, understanding the principles of user-centered design and applying best practices for simplicity, consistency, and usability is key to creating an app that users love.

By learning from successful apps like Instagram, Uber, and Khan Academy, you can apply these concepts to build your own beautiful and functional cross-platform apps. The next step is to practice these design principles and start creating UIs that will provide the best possible experience for your users.

CHAPTER 8

DATA MANAGEMENT AND STORAGE SOLUTIONS

In this chapter, we'll explore various strategies for managing and storing data in cross-platform applications. Data management is a critical component of any app, as it directly affects the user experience and performance. Whether you're storing data locally on the device or syncing it to the cloud, it's essential to choose the right solution for your app's needs. We will cover local databases, cloud storage options, and how to manage data across platforms using SQLite, Firebase, and SQL databases.

Local Databases vs Cloud Storage

Local Databases:

Local databases are stored directly on the user's device, and they allow apps to function even when the device is offline. These databases are ideal for apps that need to store data quickly, allow users to access data without a network connection, or handle sensitive information that should remain local.

Advantages of Local Databases:

- **Offline Access:** Data can be accessed and modified even without an internet connection.
- **Performance:** Local databases tend to be faster since data retrieval and writing occur directly on the device.
- **Security:** Sensitive information is kept on the user's device, reducing the risks associated with transmitting data over the internet.

Disadvantages of Local Databases:

- **Storage Limitations:** Mobile devices have limited storage space, so local databases are suitable for smaller datasets.
- **Data Syncing:** If the user switches devices or reinstalls the app, syncing data can be problematic.

Cloud Storage:

Cloud storage, on the other hand, stores data on remote servers that can be accessed via the internet. This solution is ideal for apps that need to sync data between devices, share data across users, or store large amounts of data that exceed local device storage capabilities.

Advantages of Cloud Storage:

- **Data Syncing:** Cloud storage allows data to be synchronized across multiple devices and platforms, ensuring that users always have access to their latest information.
- **Scalability:** Cloud storage can handle large datasets, and users are not limited by the device's storage capacity.
- **Accessibility:** Data is accessible from any device with internet access, making it easier to build apps with global users.

Disadvantages of Cloud Storage:

- **Internet Dependency:** Accessing data requires an internet connection, which can be problematic for users in low-connectivity areas.
- **Latency:** Cloud-based storage can introduce some latency in retrieving or uploading data, especially if the app requires real-time access.

Managing Data Across Platforms with SQLite, Firebase, and SQL Databases

1. SQLite (Local Database):

SQLite is a self-contained, serverless, and zero-configuration SQL database engine. It is a great choice for local storage in cross-platform apps, providing a reliable, lightweight solution for managing data on mobile devices.

How to Use SQLite:

- SQLite is supported natively by most mobile platforms (iOS, Android), and there are libraries available for integration with other platforms.
- SQLite is often used for storing small to medium-sized datasets like user preferences, offline data, and app settings.

Python Example (using SQLite with Kivy):

```python
python

import sqlite3

# Connect to SQLite database (it will create a
new file if it doesn't exist)
conn = sqlite3.connect('todo.db')
```

```
cursor = conn.cursor()

# Create a table for storing tasks
cursor.execute('''
CREATE TABLE IF NOT EXISTS tasks (
    id INTEGER PRIMARY KEY AUTOINCREMENT,
    task TEXT NOT NULL,
    completed BOOLEAN NOT NULL
)
''')

# Insert a task into the table
cursor.execute('INSERT    INTO    tasks    (task,
completed) VALUES (?, ?)', ('Finish homework',
False))
conn.commit()

# Retrieve all tasks
cursor.execute('SELECT * FROM tasks')
tasks = cursor.fetchall()

# Display tasks
for task in tasks:
    print(task)

# Close the connection
conn.close()
```

This example shows how to create a simple local SQLite database to store tasks in a to-do list app. The app will work offline, and data will be stored locally on the device.

---

2. Firebase (Cloud Storage):

Firebase is a platform developed by Google that provides a set of cloud services, including a real-time NoSQL database, authentication, analytics, and more. Firebase is an excellent choice for building mobile apps with real-time syncing and cloud storage.

How to Use Firebase:

- Firebase's **Cloud Firestore** is its scalable, flexible database solution. You can store data in a NoSQL format, which makes it easy to sync and store data across multiple devices.
- Firebase also provides **Firebase Authentication**, which simplifies user login and authentication for cross-platform apps.

Python Example (using Firebase): To use Firebase in Python, you can use the **firebase-admin** SDK.

```bash
bash

pip install firebase-admin
```

```python
python

import firebase_admin
from firebase_admin import credentials, firestore

# Initialize Firebase app
cred = credentials.Certificate("path_to_your_service_account_key.json")
firebase_admin.initialize_app(cred)

# Get Firestore client
db = firestore.client()

# Add a task to Firestore
task_ref = db.collection("tasks").document("task1")
task_ref.set({
    "task": "Finish homework",
    "completed": False
})

# Retrieve all tasks
tasks_ref = db.collection("tasks")
for task in tasks_ref.stream():
```

```
print(f"{task.id} => {task.to_dict()}")
```

This example shows how to add and retrieve tasks from Firebase's Firestore database, allowing for real-time data syncing across multiple devices.

Firebase Advantages:

- Real-time database updates allow for automatic syncing of data across devices without needing manual intervention.
- Built-in authentication and security rules make it easier to handle user data.

---

3. **SQL Databases (MySQL, PostgreSQL, etc.):**

SQL databases like **MySQL** and **PostgreSQL** are more traditional relational databases and can be used for cloud-based storage solutions. These databases are ideal for large, structured datasets and enterprise-level applications that require robust querying and transactional support.

How to Use SQL Databases in Cloud:

- Typically, SQL databases are hosted on cloud platforms such as AWS (RDS), Google Cloud SQL, or Azure SQL

Database. These databases are accessible via APIs over the internet and can be integrated into mobile and web apps.

- For mobile apps, you can use a **REST API** to interact with your SQL database, providing endpoints for data retrieval and manipulation.

Example: Let's assume you are using **PostgreSQL** in the cloud. Your mobile app will interact with the database via an API. Here's how the API might look:

- **GET /tasks**: Retrieve all tasks from the database.
- **POST /tasks**: Create a new task and store it in the database.
- **DELETE /tasks/{id}**: Delete a task by its ID.

You can use frameworks like **Flask** (Python) or **ASP.NET Core** (C#) to create the backend API that communicates with the SQL database.

Real-World Examples of Handling Data in Cross-Platform Apps

1. **Spotify (SQLite and Firebase):** Spotify uses **SQLite** for local data storage on mobile devices, such as caching playlists and songs for offline

listening. Firebase is used for real-time syncing of user data, playlists, and preferences across devices, ensuring users can access their data from any device without losing their settings.

2. **WhatsApp (SQL and Firebase):** WhatsApp uses a combination of **SQL** (for message storage on local devices) and **Firebase** (for real-time syncing of messages across devices). Messages are stored in local databases (like SQLite) to allow offline use, and as soon as the app connects to the internet, the data is synced across devices using Firebase's real-time database.

3. **Airbnb (Firebase and SQL):** Airbnb uses **Firebase** for real-time booking updates, enabling users to view and book properties without delay. The app also uses **SQL databases** for storing user data, listings, and transaction histories, allowing for complex queries and analytics.

Summary

Choosing the right data management and storage solution is essential for building cross-platform apps that are efficient, scalable, and provide a seamless user experience. Whether you're using **SQLite** for local storage, **Firebase** for real-time cloud syncing, or **SQL databases** for more complex cloud solutions, each option has its strengths and use cases.

By understanding how to manage and sync data across platforms, you can ensure your app is both functional and efficient, offering users a smooth experience no matter where they are or which device they use.

CHAPTER 9

NETWORKING AND APIS IN CROSS-PLATFORM DEVELOPMENT

In this chapter, we'll explore how to work with APIs (Application Programming Interfaces) and web services in cross-platform development. APIs are essential for connecting mobile apps with external services, allowing you to fetch data, send requests, and handle responses from web servers. We will cover how to make HTTP requests and handle responses in both **Python** and **C#**, and we'll also look at real-world examples of APIs being used in cross-platform applications.

Working with APIs and Web Services in Python and C#

APIs enable your application to communicate with other systems over the internet. In cross-platform app development, APIs are often used for tasks like retrieving user data, making payments, interacting with cloud services, and more.

1. Working with APIs in Python:

Python provides several libraries for making HTTP requests and working with web services. One of the most commonly used libraries is **requests**, which simplifies sending HTTP requests and handling responses.

- **Installing requests:** First, you'll need to install the requests library if it's not already installed:

bash

```
pip install requests
```

- **Making a GET Request:** You can use the requests library to fetch data from an API using a GET request. Here's a simple example of making a request to the **JSONPlaceholder API**, which provides fake data for testing.

python

```
import requests
```

```
url                                      =
"https://jsonplaceholder.typicode.com/pos
ts"

# Sending a GET request
response = requests.get(url)

if response.status_code == 200:
    # Successfully received data
    data = response.json()  # Convert JSON
response to a Python dictionary
    for post in data:
        print(f"Title: {post['title']}")
else:
    print(f"Failed to fetch data. Status
code: {response.status_code}")
```

- **Making a POST Request:** To send data to an API, you can use a POST request. Here's an example where we send new data to the API:

```python

import requests

url                                      =
"https://jsonplaceholder.typicode.com/pos
ts"
new_post = {
```

```
    "title": "New Post",
    "body": "This is the content of the new
post.",
    "userId": 1
}


response        =       requests.post(url,
json=new_post)


if response.status_code == 201:
    print("Successfully   created   a   new
post")
else:
    print(f"Failed to create post. Status
code: {response.status_code}")
```

- **Handling Errors:** You should always check for potential errors when working with APIs. Use `try-except` blocks to handle exceptions, such as timeouts, connection errors, or invalid responses.

```
python


try:
    response = requests.get(url)
    response.raise_for_status()    #  Will
raise an HTTPError if the status code is
4xx/5xx
```

```
except    requests.exceptions.HTTPError    as
err:
    print(f"HTTP error occurred: {err}")
except
requests.exceptions.RequestException    as
err:
    print(f"Error occurred: {err}")
```

2. Working with APIs in C#:

In C#, working with APIs is typically done using the **HttpClient** class, which is part of the **System.Net.Http** namespace. It provides methods for sending HTTP requests and receiving HTTP responses from a resource identified by a URI.

- **Making a GET Request:** Here's how you can make a GET request to fetch data from an API.

csharp

```csharp
using System;
using System.Net.Http;
using System.Threading.Tasks;

class Program
{
```

```
static async Task Main(string[] args)
{
    using (HttpClient client = new
HttpClient())
    {
        string url =
"https://jsonplaceholder.typicode.com/pos
ts";

        HttpResponseMessage response =
await client.GetAsync(url);
        if
(response.IsSuccessStatusCode)
        {
            string data = await
response.Content.ReadAsStringAsync();
            Console.WriteLine(data);
// Print the JSON response
        }
        else
        {
            Console.WriteLine("Failed
to retrieve data");
        }
    }
}
```

- **Making a POST Request:** To send data to an API with a POST request in C#, you can use the **PostAsync** method.

```csharp
using System;
using System.Net.Http;
using System.Text;
using System.Threading.Tasks;

class Program
{
    static async Task Main(string[] args)
    {
        using (HttpClient client = new HttpClient())
        {
            string url = "https://jsonplaceholder.typicode.com/posts";
            string json = "{\"title\":\"New Post\",\"body\":\"This is the content.\",\"userId\":1}";
            StringContent content = new StringContent(json, Encoding.UTF8, "application/json");
```

```
            HttpResponseMessage response =
await client.PostAsync(url, content);
        if
(response.IsSuccessStatusCode)
        {

Console.WriteLine("Successfully     created
post");
        }
        else
        {
            Console.WriteLine("Failed
to create post");
        }
    }
  }
}
```

- **Handling Errors:** In C#, handle potential API errors by checking the **IsSuccessStatusCode** property of the **HttpResponseMessage** object, which indicates if the HTTP response status code is in the 2xx range.

Making HTTP Requests and Handling Responses

When working with APIs, it's important to handle different HTTP methods (GET, POST, PUT, DELETE), manage request parameters, and properly handle the responses.

- **GET Requests:** Used to retrieve data from an API.
- **POST Requests:** Used to send data to an API (e.g., creating a new resource).
- **PUT Requests:** Used to update existing data on the server.
- **DELETE Requests:** Used to remove a resource from the server.

Handling Responses:

- **200 OK:** Request was successful, and the response contains the requested data.
- **201 Created:** Successfully created a new resource (typically from a POST request).
- **400 Bad Request:** The request was invalid or malformed.
- **404 Not Found:** The resource could not be found on the server.
- **500 Internal Server Error:** Something went wrong on the server side.

Always ensure you check for these status codes in your response handling to ensure the proper flow of your app.

Real-World Applications of APIs in Cross-Platform Apps

APIs are used extensively in cross-platform apps to connect with external systems and enable powerful features. Here are a few real-world examples:

1. **Social Media Integration (Facebook, Twitter, Instagram):**
   - o Many cross-platform apps use APIs to integrate with social media platforms. For example, an app might allow users to log in via Facebook or Twitter using OAuth authentication. Apps can also post content or retrieve user data from these platforms using the respective APIs.

2. **Payment Processing (Stripe, PayPal):**
   - o APIs from services like **Stripe** and **PayPal** are used in mobile apps to handle payment processing. When a user makes a purchase, the app sends payment details to the payment provider's API, which processes the transaction and returns a success or failure response.

3. **Weather Apps (OpenWeatherMap, WeatherStack):**
   - Many weather apps use APIs to fetch real-time weather data. For example, **OpenWeatherMap** provides an API that allows developers to access weather forecasts, current conditions, and other relevant data to display in their apps.

4. **Messaging Apps (Twilio):**
   - **Twilio** provides APIs that allow apps to send SMS, make phone calls, and even facilitate video calls. This API is commonly used in customer support apps, appointment reminders, and any service that requires messaging functionality.

5. **Real-Time Collaboration (Google Firebase):**
   - Apps like **Google Docs** and **Slack** rely heavily on real-time communication APIs. Firebase's **Realtime Database** and **Cloud Firestore** provide APIs that sync data across devices, allowing multiple users to edit documents or chat in real-time.

Summary

In this chapter, we covered how to interact with APIs in both **Python** and **C#**, using tools like **requests** in Python and **HttpClient** in C#. We also discussed how to make HTTP requests, handle responses, and deal with errors. Finally, we explored real-world applications of APIs in cross-platform development, showing how APIs enable essential features like social media integration, payment processing, weather data retrieval, messaging, and real-time collaboration.

Understanding how to work with APIs is crucial for building modern cross-platform applications that integrate with external systems and provide users with dynamic, feature-rich experiences.

CHAPTER 10

HANDLING USER AUTHENTICATION AND SECURITY

User authentication and data security are critical components in modern cross-platform applications. Ensuring that only authorized users can access sensitive information and resources is vital for maintaining the integrity and trustworthiness of an app. In this chapter, we will discuss the importance of security in cross-platform applications, explore popular techniques for user authentication (such as OAuth and JWT), and look at real-world examples of secure authentication systems.

Importance of Security in Cross-Platform Applications

Security is paramount in all types of applications, especially in cross-platform apps that may handle a wide variety of sensitive data, such as personal information, financial details, or proprietary business data. When apps are deployed across different platforms (iOS, Android, Web, etc.), they face additional security challenges such as maintaining consistent security policies across platforms, securing communication between devices, and handling third-party integrations.

Here are key reasons why security is essential in cross-platform applications:

1. **Data Protection:** Protecting users' sensitive data (e.g., login credentials, personal details, financial information) from unauthorized access is critical. Breaches can lead to identity theft, fraud, and loss of customer trust.

2. **Maintaining User Privacy:** With stricter privacy regulations (such as GDPR and CCPA), apps must be designed to protect users' private information and comply with legal requirements.

3. **Preventing Unauthorized Access:** If an app does not authenticate users correctly, it can lead to unauthorized users gaining access to restricted content or features, which could result in data leaks or malicious actions.

4. **Cross-Platform Consistency:** Since cross-platform apps need to work across various operating systems

and devices, ensuring security features like user authentication and data encryption are consistent across platforms is crucial.

5. **Defending Against Cyber Attacks:** Cross-platform apps are often targeted by hackers. Protecting against threats like cross-site scripting (XSS), cross-site request forgery (CSRF), SQL injection, and man-in-the-middle (MITM) attacks is necessary to safeguard both the app and its users.

Techniques for User Authentication: OAuth and JWT

1. OAuth (Open Authorization)

OAuth is a widely used open standard for access delegation. It allows third-party applications to access user data without exposing the user's credentials (e.g., username and password). OAuth is often used to grant access to APIs securely and is commonly used for login services (e.g., "Login with Google", "Login with Facebook").

How OAuth Works:

- **Authorization Grant:** OAuth starts with the user granting permission to a third-party app (the client) to access their resources. This is done by redirecting the user to the authorization server (e.g., Google, Facebook).

- **Access Token:** Once the user grants permission, the authorization server issues an access token to the client. The client then uses this token to access protected resources on the server.

- **Refresh Token (optional):** Some OAuth implementations also provide a refresh token, which allows the client to obtain a new access token without needing the user to authenticate again.

Example Use Case:

- "Login with Google" allows users to sign in to an app without creating a new password. After the user grants permission, the app receives an OAuth access token, which it can use to access the user's Google account information (e.g., email, profile data).

2. JWT (JSON Web Token)

JSON Web Tokens (JWT) is an open standard for securely transmitting information between parties as a JSON object. It is commonly used in authentication systems to ensure the integrity and authenticity of the data being sent. JWTs can be used to implement stateless authentication, where the server doesn't need to store session data. Instead, the token itself contains all the necessary information to authenticate a user.

How JWT Works:

- **Login:** The user logs in with their credentials (e.g., username and password). If the credentials are valid, the server generates a JWT and sends it back to the client.
- **Token Storage:** The client stores the JWT (usually in local storage or as a cookie).
- **Subsequent Requests:** For subsequent requests, the client sends the JWT in the `Authorization` header (typically as a Bearer token) to authenticate the request.
- **Token Validation:** The server validates the JWT's signature and, if valid, allows access to protected resources.

JWT Structure:

- **Header:** Contains metadata about the token, including the signing algorithm.
- **Payload:** Contains the claims (e.g., user information, roles, permissions).
- **Signature:** Ensures the integrity of the token by allowing the server to verify that it hasn't been tampered with.

Example Use Case:

- A mobile app allows users to log in via email and password. After successful login, the app receives a JWT, which it uses for subsequent API calls to access user data securely.

Advantages of JWT:

- **Stateless Authentication:** No need to store session information on the server.
- **Scalability:** Ideal for distributed or microservice architectures.
- **Self-Contained:** The JWT contains all necessary user data (e.g., user ID, roles) and can be verified without accessing a database.

Real-World Examples of Secure Authentication Systems

1. **Google OAuth (OAuth 2.0):**
   - Google uses OAuth 2.0 to allow users to log in to third-party apps using their Google credentials. By authenticating via Google, users don't need to create new passwords for every app, and the app gets an access token to fetch the user's basic information like email or profile picture.
   - For example, apps like **Slack** or **Trello** allow users to log in with their Google account. The app

108

receives an OAuth token and uses it to access user data securely.

2. **JWT in APIs (e.g., REST APIs):**

   o Many modern APIs, including social media APIs (like **Facebook Graph API**) and cloud services (like **AWS API Gateway**), use **JWT** to authenticate and authorize users.

   o **Auth0**, a popular authentication service, provides a platform for managing JWT-based authentication. Apps like **Spotify** and **Netflix** use JWT to securely authenticate users and manage sessions across multiple platforms (mobile, desktop, web).

3. **Facebook Login (OAuth 2.0):**

   o Facebook's **Login API** allows developers to integrate Facebook login functionality in their apps. It uses OAuth 2.0, allowing users to authenticate via Facebook without sharing their password with the third-party app.

   o Many apps like **Spotify**, **Airbnb**, and **Instagram** use Facebook login to authenticate users.

4. **Amazon (JWT & OAuth):**

   o **Amazon Web Services (AWS)** uses a combination of **JWT** and **OAuth** to manage API access and authentication across its services. For example, when using **AWS Lambda** with **API**

Gateway, JWT is used to authenticate users and authorize them to access specific resources in the cloud.

5. **GitHub OAuth Authentication:**

   o   **GitHub** allows users to authenticate with OAuth, enabling third-party apps like **Travis CI** or **Heroku** to interact with a user's GitHub repositories securely. Once authenticated, these apps can access the user's repositories, commits, and issues based on the OAuth token permissions.

Summary

Authentication and security are integral to the success of any cross-platform application. By using established techniques like **OAuth** for secure third-party authentication and **JWT** for managing stateless authentication, developers can ensure that their apps are both secure and user-friendly.

Real-world examples like **Google OAuth**, **JWT-based authentication** in APIs, and **Facebook Login** illustrate how these authentication systems are used in modern apps. By understanding these methods and implementing them correctly, you can safeguard your users' data and build a secure, scalable cross-platform app that inspires trust.

CHAPTER 11

OPTIMIZING PERFORMANCE IN CROSS-PLATFORM APPS

Performance optimization is crucial in cross-platform app development. Users expect fast, responsive applications, regardless of the platform they are using. Whether you're building a mobile app for iOS and Android or a web app that runs on multiple browsers, optimizing performance ensures that your app delivers a smooth experience, minimizes battery usage, and utilizes device resources efficiently. In this chapter, we'll cover techniques for improving app performance across platforms, how to profile and optimize code in **Python** and **C#**, and real-world optimization challenges and solutions.

Techniques for Improving App Performance Across Platforms

1. **Optimize Rendering and UI Performance:**
   - **Limit Unnecessary Re-renders:** In cross-platform UI frameworks like **React Native** or **Xamarin.Forms**, unnecessary UI re-renders can

slow down your app. Use lifecycle methods like `shouldComponentUpdate` in React Native or `OnPropertyChanged` in Xamarin to ensure that only relevant UI elements are updated.

- o **Use Lazy Loading:** For apps that load large amounts of data, use lazy loading to only load content as needed. For example, in mobile apps, only load the items visible to the user on the screen and load the rest in the background.

- o **Optimize Animations and Transitions:** Ensure that animations are smooth by minimizing the complexity of transitions and avoiding large image assets that slow down the app. Frameworks like **Xamarin.Forms** and **Kivy** offer optimizations like GPU acceleration for smoother animations.

2. **Efficient Memory Management:**

- o **Reduce Memory Usage:** Unused resources, such as images or data objects, should be disposed of properly to avoid memory leaks. Use memory profiling tools to detect memory usage spikes and take action to reduce unnecessary memory consumption.

- o **Use Object Pooling:** For apps with intensive memory requirements, implement object pooling to reuse objects instead of constantly creating new ones, which can improve performance and reduce the load on garbage collection.

3. **Optimize Network Requests:**

   o **Minimize API Calls:** Reduce the number of API calls by batching requests or implementing caching to store frequent API responses. For example, cache data locally to avoid making repeated calls to the server.

   o **Use Efficient Data Formats:** When sending data over the network, choose compact and fast data formats such as **JSON** or **Protocol Buffers** instead of heavier formats like XML.

   o **Async and Parallel Requests:** In both mobile and web apps, perform network operations asynchronously or in parallel to avoid blocking the main thread and to improve responsiveness.

4. **Use Background Tasks and Multithreading:**

   o **Background Processing:** For tasks that require significant computation (e.g., image processing, file uploads), offload these operations to background tasks or worker threads. This ensures that the main thread remains responsive to user input.

   o **Multithreading:** In **C#**, you can use the **Task Parallel Library (TPL)** to execute CPU-bound tasks in parallel, thus improving the app's performance on multi-core processors. In **Python**, use the `threading` module for multithreading, but be mindful of the Global Interpreter Lock (GIL) when dealing with CPU-bound tasks.

Profiling and Optimizing Code in Python and C#

1. Profiling Code in Python:

Profiling helps identify parts of your code that are bottlenecks, allowing you to focus optimization efforts where they are most needed. Python provides several tools for profiling and optimizing code.

- **Using `cProfile` for Profiling:** The `cProfile` module is built into Python and provides detailed reports on the time spent in each function.

```python
python

import cProfile

def my_function():
    # Some computationally intensive code
    pass
```

```
cProfile.run('my_function()')
```

This will output a detailed report showing which functions took the most time during execution.

- **Using `time` for Simple Performance Measurement:** For simpler performance checks, use the `time` module to measure the execution time of different sections of your code.

```python
import time

start_time = time.time()
# Code to measure
end_time = time.time()

print(f"Execution time:   {end_time -
start_time} seconds")
```

- **Optimizing Common Python Bottlenecks:**
  - **Avoiding Global Variables:** Access to global variables can be slower than local variables, so minimize their usage.
  - **Using List Comprehensions:** Python's list comprehensions are faster than using regular loops, so use them whenever possible.

116

o **Using Built-in Functions:** Built-in Python functions, like `sum()` and `sorted()`, are highly optimized and should be used instead of writing custom solutions.

2. Profiling Code in C#:

C# provides several powerful tools for profiling code and optimizing performance. The most commonly used tools are Visual Studio's built-in profiler and the **dotTrace** profiler.

- **Using Visual Studio Profiler:** Visual Studio comes with a built-in profiler that allows you to analyze CPU usage, memory usage, and thread activity.
  - o **Step 1:** Open the "Diagnostic Tools" window.
  - o **Step 2:** Start debugging your app.
  - o **Step 3:** Use the profiler to capture data on CPU usage and memory allocation.
  - o **Step 4:** Look for hot spots or bottlenecks in your application.
- **Using BenchmarkDotNet for Performance Testing: BenchmarkDotNet** is a library that helps you measure the performance of C# code with high accuracy.

117

```
csharp

using BenchmarkDotNet.Attributes;
using BenchmarkDotNet.Running;

public class MyBenchmark
{
    [Benchmark]
    public void MyMethod()
    {
        // Code to benchmark
    }
}

public static void Main(string[] args)
{
    var            summary            =
BenchmarkRunner.Run<MyBenchmark>();
}
```

BenchmarkDotNet will provide you with detailed results, allowing you to identify performance bottlenecks.

- **Optimizing Common C# Bottlenecks:**
  - o **Avoiding String Concatenation in Loops:** Use StringBuilder for string manipulation inside loops, as repeated string concatenation can lead to performance issues due to memory allocation.

118

o **Using Value Types (Structs) for Small Objects:** For small objects, consider using value types (structs) instead of reference types (classes) to avoid memory overhead from heap allocation.

o **Efficient Data Structures:** Use the right data structure for the task. For example, use **Dictionary** or **HashSet** for quick lookups instead of lists.

Real-World Optimization Challenges and Solutions

1. **Optimizing Large Data Sets in a Mobile App (e.g., Instagram):**

    o **Challenge:** Instagram's mobile app has to handle millions of posts, images, and videos. Efficiently loading, displaying, and caching this data is crucial for performance.

    o **Solution:** Instagram uses **lazy loading** to only load the posts that are visible on the user's screen. The app also uses **image caching** to avoid downloading images every time the user scrolls through their feed.

2. **Reducing Latency in Real-Time Communication (e.g., WhatsApp):**

- o **Challenge:** WhatsApp requires real-time message delivery, which means every message must be sent and received instantly.

- o **Solution:** WhatsApp uses efficient **WebSocket** connections to maintain a persistent connection with the server, minimizing latency. It also compresses messages and attachments to reduce network overhead.

3. **Optimizing Search and Query Performance in a Web App (e.g., Airbnb):**

- o **Challenge:** Airbnb's search functionality must be fast, even with a large number of listings and users.

- o **Solution:** Airbnb uses **Elasticsearch**, a distributed search engine, to handle large-scale search queries efficiently. It also caches frequently searched results to reduce load times for users.

4. **Optimizing Battery Usage in a Mobile App (e.g., Uber):**

- o **Challenge:** Uber's app needs to track the user's location in real time, which can drain the battery quickly.

- o **Solution:** Uber optimizes battery usage by **adjusting location tracking intervals** and using **background services** to track the user's location only when necessary, instead of constantly updating in real time.

Summary

Optimizing performance in cross-platform apps is critical to providing a seamless, fast, and responsive user experience. Techniques such as optimizing rendering, memory usage, network requests, and implementing background tasks are essential for improving app performance. Profiling and analyzing your code in **Python** and **C#** allows you to pinpoint bottlenecks and improve efficiency. Real-world optimization challenges like those faced by **Instagram**, **WhatsApp**, **Airbnb**, and **Uber** highlight the importance of performance optimization in building successful, scalable apps.

By applying these strategies and tools, you can ensure that your cross-platform app performs well on all devices and platforms, providing users with a smooth experience that meets their expectations.

CHAPTER 12

DEBUGGING AND TESTING CROSS-PLATFORM APPS

In this chapter, we'll discuss the common bugs and errors that developers encounter in cross-platform development, explore best practices for debugging and error handling in **Python** and **C#**, and cover how to write unit and integration tests using popular tools. Effective debugging and testing are critical to delivering a robust, high-performance app that works well across all platforms.

Common Bugs and Errors in Cross-Platform Development

Cross-platform development introduces unique challenges because the app needs to run seamlessly across different operating systems and devices (e.g., Android, iOS, macOS, Windows). Some common bugs and errors in cross-platform apps include:

1. **UI Inconsistencies:**

o   **Problem:** UI components may look or behave differently on different platforms due to differences in rendering engines or the way platforms handle native controls.

o   **Solution:** Test your app thoroughly on all target platforms. Use platform-specific styling or conditional rendering to ensure the UI behaves consistently across devices. For example, in **React Native**, you can use the `Platform` module to apply platform-specific styles.

2. **Device-Specific Bugs:**

o   **Problem:** A feature may work on one device but fail on another due to differences in hardware, screen size, or OS version.

o   **Solution:** Always test on a variety of devices and OS versions to ensure compatibility. Use emulators and simulators for initial testing but also perform tests on physical devices to catch device-specific issues.

3. **Networking Issues:**

o   **Problem:** API calls may work on one platform but fail on another due to differences in network configurations, timeouts, or security settings.

o   **Solution:** Ensure that the app handles network connectivity issues gracefully. Use retries,

123

timeouts, and proper error handling when making HTTP requests.

4. **Concurrency Problems:**

   o **Problem:** Issues can arise when multiple processes or threads are trying to access shared resources, such as database access or UI elements, at the same time.

   o **Solution:** Use proper synchronization mechanisms, such as locks or semaphores, to avoid concurrency issues. In **C#**, you can use `async` and `await` for asynchronous programming, and in **Python**, you can use `threading` and `asyncio` for handling concurrency.

5. **Data Persistence Problems:**

   o **Problem:** Inconsistent or incorrect data storage and retrieval across different platforms, especially when using local databases (e.g., SQLite) or cloud-based storage (e.g., Firebase).

   o **Solution:** Ensure consistent data models across platforms. Use proper data validation and serialization to guarantee that data is correctly saved and loaded from local and remote storage.

Best Practices for Debugging and Error Handling in Python and C#

1. Debugging in Python:

- ## Using Built-in Debugging Tools:
    - o Python comes with a built-in debugger called **pdb** (Python Debugger). You can set breakpoints and step through your code to investigate the program's state.

```python
import pdb
pdb.set_trace()  # Set a breakpoint
```

This will pause the program execution and allow you to inspect variables, evaluate expressions, and step through the code interactively.

- ## Using IDE Debuggers:
    - o Modern Integrated Development Environments (IDEs) such as **PyCharm** and **VS Code** have built-in debuggers that allow you to set breakpoints, inspect variables, and step through code visually.

- ## Logging and Error Handling:

o Use the **logging** module to log important events and errors in your app. It's more flexible and better suited for production than using print() statements.

```python

import logging

logging.basicConfig(level=logging.DEBUG)

def my_function():
    logging.debug("This    is    a    debug message")
    logging.error("This    is    an    error message")

my_function()
```

This will log the messages, including errors, to the console or a file, which is especially useful for troubleshooting in production.

- **Handling Exceptions:**
    o Use try-except blocks to catch and handle exceptions gracefully. This allows the app to recover from errors without crashing.

126

```python
python

try:
    # Code that might throw an exception
    result = 10 / 0
except ZeroDivisionError as e:
    logging.error(f"Error occurred: {e}")
```

2. Debugging in C#:

- **Using Visual Studio Debugger:**
    - o Visual Studio provides a powerful debugger that allows you to set breakpoints, step through code, inspect variables, and evaluate expressions in a graphical interface. You can also use features like **Watch, Immediate Window**, and **Call Stack** to understand your app's state.
- **Logging in C#:**
    - o Use the built-in **ILogger** interface for logging messages in your application. This is especially useful for debugging and monitoring your app in production.

```csharp
csharp

using Microsoft.Extensions.Logging;
```

```
public class MyClass
{
    private    readonly    ILogger<MyClass>
_logger;

    public          MyClass(ILogger<MyClass>
logger)
    {
        _logger = logger;
    }

    public void DoWork()
    {
        _logger.LogDebug("Starting work");
        _logger.LogError("An          error
occurred");
    }
}
```

- **Handling Exceptions:**
  - o Use `try-catch` blocks in **C#** to handle
    exceptions and prevent your app from crashing
    unexpectedly.

```
csharp

try
{
    int result = 10 / 0;
```

```
}
catch (DivideByZeroException ex)
{
    Console.WriteLine($"Error:
{ex.Message}");
}
```

- **Debugging with Profilers:**
  - o Use tools like **dotTrace** (for performance profiling) or **Visual Studio's Diagnostic Tools** to analyze CPU and memory usage and identify performance bottlenecks.

Writing Unit and Integration Tests Using Popular Tools

1. Unit Testing in Python:

- **Using `unittest`:** Python's built-in `unittest` module allows you to write unit tests for individual functions or methods.

```python
import unittest

def add(a, b):
    return a + b
```

```
class
TestMathFunctions(unittest.TestCase):
    def test_add(self):
        self.assertEqual(add(2, 3), 5)
        self.assertEqual(add(-1, 1), 0)

if __name__ == "__main__":
    unittest.main()
```

- **Using pytest: pytest** is a more advanced testing framework that provides a simpler syntax, supports fixtures, and is widely used in the Python community.

```python
python

import pytest

def add(a, b):
    return a + b

def test_add():
    assert add(2, 3) == 5
    assert add(-1, 1) == 0
```

To run the tests, simply run pytest from the command line.

2. Unit Testing in C#:

- **Using xUnit: xUnit** is a popular testing framework for C# that is commonly used in .NET applications. It allows you to write unit tests using a simple and expressive syntax.

```csharp
public class MathFunctions
{
    public int Add(int a, int b)
    {
        return a + b;
    }
}

public class MathFunctionsTests
{
    [Fact]
    public void Add_ReturnsCorrectSum()
    {
        var math = new MathFunctions();
        var result = math.Add(2, 3);
        Assert.Equal(5, result);
    }
}
```

- **Using MSTest: MSTest** is another unit testing framework in C# that is integrated with Visual Studio. It allows you to write tests in a similar manner to **xUnit**.

csharp

```
[TestClass]
public class MathFunctionsTests
{
    [TestMethod]
    public void Add_ReturnsCorrectSum()
    {
        var math = new MathFunctions();
        var result = math.Add(2, 3);
        Assert.AreEqual(5, result);
    }
}
```

3. Integration Testing:

- **Integration Testing in Python:** Integration tests ensure that multiple components or systems work together as expected. Use **unittest** or **pytest** with mock objects or real services to test the interaction between different parts of the system (e.g., database interactions, API calls).

- **Integration Testing in C#:** In C#, you can use **MSTest** or **xUnit** for integration testing, along with tools like **Microsoft's `TestServer`** to simulate HTTP requests and responses for web APIs, or **Entity Framework Core In-Memory Database** to test database interactions.

Summary

Debugging and testing are essential for ensuring that your cross-platform apps run smoothly and reliably across different devices and platforms. By following best practices for error handling and using powerful debugging tools, you can quickly identify and resolve issues. Writing unit and integration tests ensures that your app behaves as expected and that changes do not introduce new bugs. Whether you're using **Python** or **C#**, these practices and tools will help you deliver high-quality apps that are robust, secure, and performant.

CHAPTER 13

DEPLOYING AND DISTRIBUTING CROSS-PLATFORM APPS

Deploying and distributing your cross-platform application is the final step in the development lifecycle. After building your app, you need to ensure it's accessible to users on their respective platforms (iOS, Android, Web, etc.). In this chapter, we'll cover deployment strategies for both **Python** and **C#** applications, discuss how to publish your app to app stores, servers, or cloud platforms, and provide real-world examples of successful app deployments.

Deployment Strategies for Python and C# Applications

1. Deployment Strategies for Python Applications:

Python is often used for backend services, web applications, or scripting. There are several strategies for deploying Python applications depending on the use case (web app, desktop app, or script).

- **For Web Applications:**
  - o **Cloud Platforms (e.g., AWS, Heroku, Google Cloud):** Cloud platforms like **AWS Elastic Beanstalk**, **Heroku**, or **Google App Engine** are popular choices for deploying Python web apps. These platforms handle the infrastructure for you, allowing you to focus on your app.
    - **Heroku:** With a simple command-line tool, you can deploy Python applications to **Heroku** with minimal configuration.

```bash
git push heroku master   # Push your app to Heroku
```

  - o **Virtual Private Servers (VPS):** If you want more control over the server environment, you can use services like **DigitalOcean** or **Linode** to deploy your Python application. You can configure the server with tools like **Gunicorn** for serving the app and **nginx** as a reverse proxy.
  - o **Containers (Docker):** Containerization allows you to package your Python app with

135

its dependencies and deploy it anywhere that supports Docker. This approach is widely used in production systems because it ensures consistency across development, testing, and production environments.

```bash
docker build -t my-python-app .
docker run -d -p 5000:5000 my-python-app  # Run the container on port 5000
```

- **For Desktop Applications:**
  - o **PyInstaller or cx_Freeze:** For cross-platform desktop applications, you can use tools like **PyInstaller** or **cx_Freeze** to bundle your Python app into an executable that can be run on various operating systems (Windows, macOS, Linux).

```bash
pyinstaller --onefile my_app.py    # Create a single executable file
```

- **For Scripts and CLI Tools:** If you're building a command-line tool or script, you can distribute it via package managers like **pip** (Python's package

136

manager) or create executable files using **PyInstaller**.

---

2. Deployment Strategies for C# Applications:

C# is commonly used for both backend services and cross-platform desktop/mobile apps (via Xamarin). The deployment strategies for C# depend on the type of application you are developing.

- **For Web Applications (ASP.NET Core):**
  - **Cloud Platforms (e.g., Azure, AWS, Google Cloud): Microsoft Azure** is the natural choice for deploying ASP.NET Core applications. However, other cloud platforms like AWS and Google Cloud can also be used to deploy C# apps.
    - **Azure App Service:** Azure provides managed services for deploying, scaling, and maintaining web apps. You can deploy directly from Visual Studio or GitHub using **Azure DevOps**.

      bash

```
az webapp up --name myapp --resource-
group myResourceGroup
```

o **Docker Containers:** Like Python, C# apps (especially ASP.NET Core apps) can be containerized and deployed on cloud platforms or on-premise servers using Docker.

```
bash
```

```
docker build -t my-dotnet-app .
docker run -d -p 5000:80 my-dotnet-
app
```

- **For Desktop Applications (WPF, WinForms, or MAUI):**
    o **Microsoft Store (Windows Apps):** If you're building a Windows desktop app with **WPF** or **WinForms**, you can publish it to the **Microsoft Store** using the **MSIX** packaging tool.
        ▪ MSIX ensures your app runs on all Windows 10 devices and handles deployment, installation, and updates automatically.

138

o **Cross-Platform Desktop Apps (MAUI, Xamarin): .NET MAUI** (Multi-platform App UI) allows you to create cross-platform applications for iOS, Android, macOS, and Windows. These apps can be deployed to app stores (Google Play Store, Apple App Store) or distributed directly to users.

```bash
dotnet publish -f:net6.0-android -c Release
```

o **Publishing .NET Desktop Apps:** If you're targeting Windows specifically, **ClickOnce** and **MSIX** are the most common ways to distribute your app. Both methods allow for seamless deployment and updating of desktop applications.

How to Publish Your App to App Stores, Servers, or Cloud Platforms

1. Publishing to App Stores:

For **mobile apps** (iOS and Android) or **cross-platform apps** like **Xamarin** or **.NET MAUI**, the process of publishing to app stores involves packaging the app and submitting it to the store.

- **Google Play Store (Android):**
  - **Generate APK or AAB:** For Android apps built with **Xamarin** or **.NET MAUI**, you can generate an APK (Android Package) or an AAB (Android App Bundle) file for submission.
  - **Upload to Google Play Console:** Once you have the APK or AAB, you can upload it to the **Google Play Console**. After approval, your app will be available on the Play Store.

```bash
dotnet publish -f:net6.0-android -c Release
```

- **Apple App Store (iOS):**
  - **Generate IPA:** For iOS apps, you'll need to generate an **IPA** (iOS App Archive) file. You can use **Xamarin** or **MAUI** for this, or use **Xcode** for native apps.

- o **Upload to App Store Connect:** Once the IPA is generated, you can upload it to **App Store Connect** for submission and approval.
  - Make sure to follow Apple's guidelines and meet their requirements for app submission.

2. Deploying to Servers:

For backend applications (Python web apps, ASP.NET Core apps), you can deploy them to a variety of servers and cloud platforms.

- **AWS, Google Cloud, or Azure:** These cloud providers offer easy-to-use services for deploying applications. You can use services like **AWS Elastic Beanstalk**, **Google App Engine**, or **Azure App Service** to deploy your web apps.
- **VPS or Dedicated Servers:** If you prefer more control over your server, you can deploy to a **VPS** (e.g., DigitalOcean, Linode) or dedicated server. You'll need to configure the server manually, install the required software (e.g., web server, database), and deploy your application.

3. Deploying to Cloud Platforms:

141

For both Python and C# apps, cloud deployment is one of the most scalable and flexible options. Common platforms include:

- **Microsoft Azure (for C#):** Azure is an ideal cloud platform for deploying **ASP.NET Core**, **MAUI**, or **Xamarin** apps. You can easily integrate Azure services such as databases, storage, and serverless functions into your app.
- **AWS (for Python and C#):** AWS provides a wide range of services for both **Python** and **C#** apps. You can deploy web applications using **AWS Elastic Beanstalk** or create serverless functions using **AWS Lambda**.
- **Google Cloud (for Python and C#):** Google Cloud offers managed services and cloud infrastructure for both Python and C# applications. You can deploy your apps to **Google App Engine** or use **Google Kubernetes Engine** for containerized apps.

Real-World Examples of Successful App Deployments

1. **Instagram (Python - Django):**

o **Deployment Strategy:** Instagram uses **Amazon Web Services (AWS)** for hosting its backend, with a combination of EC2 instances, S3 for storage, and RDS for databases.

o **Challenges and Solutions:** As Instagram grew, it faced scaling issues. The solution was to use distributed systems and content delivery networks (CDNs) to handle massive traffic loads.

2. **WhatsApp (C# - Erlang):**

o **Deployment Strategy:** WhatsApp's backend infrastructure is primarily built using **Erlang**, but it integrates with services written in **C#** for some parts. It uses **AWS** to deploy and scale its infrastructure.

o **Challenges and Solutions:** To handle billions of messages daily, WhatsApp optimized for minimal server resources and high throughput, using techniques like message queuing and load balancing.

3. **Spotify (C# - .NET Core):**

o **Deployment Strategy:** Spotify uses **AWS Elastic Beanstalk** for deployment, scaling its services using EC2 instances and S3 storage.

o **Challenges and Solutions:** Spotify uses **microservices architecture** to decouple features (e.g., music streaming, recommendations,

143

payments), allowing for independent scaling and management of services.

4. **Slack (Python - Django):**

   o **Deployment Strategy:** Slack relies on **AWS Lambda** for serverless computing and **Amazon S3** for storage. It uses a hybrid cloud model to improve scalability and reduce latency.

   o **Challenges and Solutions:** Slack's high dependency on real-time communication means minimizing downtime. Slack uses load balancing and automatic scaling to handle millions of messages per day across teams and platforms.

Summary

Deploying and distributing cross-platform applications involves selecting the right deployment strategies, tools, and platforms for your app. Whether you're deploying a Python web app to a cloud platform like **Heroku**, or a C# mobile app to the **Google Play Store**, the process requires careful planning and attention to detail. By following the steps outlined in this chapter and learning from real-world examples, you can successfully deploy your app, ensure it's scalable, and make it accessible to users across multiple platforms.

CHAPTER 14

MAINTAINING AND UPDATING CROSS-PLATFORM APPS

Once a cross-platform app is deployed and in use, maintaining its performance, ensuring regular updates, and managing its lifecycle become crucial. Continuous improvement and timely updates are key to keeping your app relevant, secure, and user-friendly across various platforms. In this chapter, we'll discuss best practices for app maintenance, version control, updating apps across multiple platforms, and real-world strategies for managing app lifecycles.

Best Practices for App Maintenance and Version Control

1. App Maintenance Best Practices:

App maintenance involves fixing bugs, updating dependencies, improving performance, and ensuring compatibility with newer operating systems and devices.

Some best practices for maintaining your cross-platform app include:

- **Regular Bug Fixes and Performance Improvements:**
  - o Continuously monitor your app for bugs and performance bottlenecks. Use **error tracking tools** like **Sentry** or **Rollbar** to track runtime exceptions and crashes across platforms.
  - o Regularly address any user-reported bugs and prioritize critical issues that impact the user experience.

- **Updating Dependencies:**
  - o Cross-platform apps often rely on third-party libraries and dependencies. Keep these libraries up to date to ensure compatibility with the latest platform versions and security fixes.
  - o Use tools like **pip** (Python) or **NuGet** (C#) to easily manage dependencies and ensure that your app remains compatible with the latest library versions.

- **Refactoring Code:**
  - o As your app evolves, regularly refactor the codebase to improve readability, modularity, and maintainability. Use automated refactoring tools to help streamline the process.

147

o Refactoring ensures that the app remains easy to maintain and that performance bottlenecks or security vulnerabilities in the code are minimized.

- **Cross-Platform Compatibility:**

    o Regularly test your app across various platforms and devices to ensure compatibility with the latest OS updates. Mobile operating systems like **iOS** and **Android** frequently update, so you must ensure your app remains functional on new versions.

    o Use emulators, simulators, and real devices for testing, and leverage **continuous integration (CI)** pipelines to automate testing and deployment.

---

2. Version Control:

Version control is essential in managing an app's source code and collaborating with other developers. Using a system like **Git** helps manage code changes, track bugs, and maintain a history of all modifications. Best practices for version control include:

- **Branching Strategies:**

148

- o Use branching strategies like **Git Flow** or **GitHub Flow** to manage development, staging, and production environments. The basic idea is to create a main branch (`master` or `main`) for production code and feature branches for new work.
- o This approach allows you to isolate features, fix bugs independently, and merge code in a controlled manner.

- **Semantic Versioning:**
  - o Adhere to **semantic versioning** to clearly communicate changes and updates to your app. Semantic versioning typically uses a format like `MAJOR.MINOR.PATCH`:
    - **MAJOR** version changes indicate backward-incompatible changes.
    - **MINOR** version changes indicate backward-compatible features.
    - **PATCH** version changes indicate backward-compatible bug fixes.

- **Commit Messages and Documentation:**
  - o Write clear and descriptive commit messages, including the reason for the change, bug fixes, and the scope of updates.
  - o Document major updates and features for future reference and collaboration. Good documentation

149

helps new developers understand the codebase and the app's functionality quickly.

Updating Apps Across Multiple Platforms

1. Managing Updates in Cross-Platform Mobile Apps:

For mobile applications, updates can be a complex process since both the **Google Play Store** and the **Apple App Store** have different submission guidelines and approval processes. Below are steps to streamline this process:

- **Automating the Build and Deployment Process:**
    - Use **CI/CD** **(Continuous Integration/Continuous Deployment)** pipelines to automate the process of building, testing, and deploying updates. Tools like **Jenkins**, **GitHub Actions**, and **Azure DevOps** allow you to automate builds and testing for both iOS and Android simultaneously.
    - For cross-platform frameworks like **Xamarin** and **Flutter**, you can automate the creation of Android APKs and iOS IPA files, and deploy them to respective app stores.
- **Versioning Your App:**

o When releasing an update, increment the version number (using semantic versioning) and make sure you update the app's metadata on both the **Google Play Store** and **Apple App Store**. Ensure that the description, changelog, and screenshots are updated to reflect new features and fixes.

o For iOS apps, the **App Store Connect** platform helps manage app versions and track update approvals. For Android, the **Google Play Console** serves a similar purpose.

- **Beta Testing Updates:**

  o Before releasing an update to the general public, use beta testing programs to identify any issues early. Platforms like **TestFlight** for iOS and **Google Play's Closed Testing** for Android allow you to distribute early versions to selected testers.

  o This step helps catch bugs and usability issues before your app is released to a broader audience.

- **In-App Updates:**

  o Implement **in-app update mechanisms** using the **Google Play In-App Update API** or **Apple's App Store Connect**. This allows users to receive app updates without going through the full app store installation process.

  o For **React Native** apps, you can use libraries like **react-native-code-push** to deploy updates

151

directly to users, without requiring an app store update.

2. Managing Updates for Web and Desktop Apps:

For web and desktop apps, updates are typically managed through web servers or desktop app distribution mechanisms.

- **Web Applications (e.g., React, Django):**
  - o For web apps, updates are deployed to the server and can be delivered instantly to users once the app is updated. Use versioning for assets (like images, CSS, and JavaScript files) to prevent caching issues.
  - o Tools like **Docker** and **Kubernetes** can help manage web app deployments at scale by providing consistent environments across different platforms.
- **Desktop Applications (e.g., .NET MAUI, Electron):**
  - o For desktop applications, distribution and updates are managed through platforms like **Microsoft Store**, **Mac App Store**, or direct downloads from the app's website.

152

o Tools like **Squirrel.Windows** (for Windows) and **Electron-Updater** (for Electron apps) allow you to create automatic update systems for desktop apps. These tools automatically download and install the latest version of the app on the user's machine.

Real-World Strategies for Managing App Lifecycles

Effective app lifecycle management is essential to ensure that your app remains functional, secure, and relevant throughout its lifetime. Here are a few real-world strategies for managing app lifecycles:

1. **Versioning and Backward Compatibility (Spotify):**
   o **Spotify** uses API versioning and backward compatibility to ensure that its app continues to work even as the backend changes. They have established versioning policies to ensure that old app versions still function while newer ones are released with new features.

2. **Continuous Monitoring and Bug Fixing (Airbnb):**
   o **Airbnb** uses **Sentry** and **New Relic** to continuously monitor app performance and detect

errors in real-time. When issues arise, they are promptly addressed in the next release, ensuring a smooth experience for users across all platforms.

3. **Rolling Updates and Blue-Green Deployment (Netflix):**

   o **Netflix** uses a blue-green deployment strategy, where new versions of the app are deployed in parallel with the existing version. This allows them to roll back quickly in case of issues. Users are gradually switched to the new version, ensuring stability.

4. **App Lifecycle Management in Cloud (Dropbox):**

   o **Dropbox** handles app versioning and lifecycle management by storing app updates in the cloud. Users are automatically updated to the latest version of the app, and rollback to previous versions can be done easily if needed.

Summary

Maintaining and updating cross-platform apps is a continuous process that requires careful planning, version control, and effective deployment strategies. By following best practices for maintenance, using version control systems, and automating the update process, you can ensure that your app remains functional, secure, and user-friendly across all platforms. Real-world examples from companies like **Spotify**, **Airbnb**, **Netflix**, and **Dropbox** demonstrate the importance of managing app lifecycles effectively, providing users with a seamless experience even as the app evolves over time.

CHAPTER 15

WORKING WITH CLOUD SERVICES AND APIS

Cloud services have become an integral part of modern cross-platform development, providing scalable, flexible, and reliable solutions for app backends. In this chapter, we'll introduce major cloud platforms like **AWS**, **Azure**, and **Google Cloud**. We'll also explore how to leverage these cloud services for building powerful backend solutions for your cross-platform apps. Finally, we'll discuss real-world examples of cloud-based apps and how they utilize these platforms for optimal performance and scalability.

Introduction to Cloud Platforms (AWS, Azure, Google Cloud)

1. AWS (Amazon Web Services):

- **Overview:** AWS is one of the most widely used cloud computing platforms, offering a comprehensive suite of services including compute, storage, databases, networking, machine learning, and more. AWS allows you to deploy scalable applications without worrying about managing physical infrastructure.

- **Key Services for App Development:**
  - o **EC2 (Elastic Compute Cloud):** Provides scalable compute capacity. You can launch virtual servers (instances) to host your app.
  - o **Lambda:** A serverless compute service that allows you to run code in response to events without provisioning or managing servers.
  - o **S3 (Simple Storage Service):** For object storage, ideal for storing images, videos, and other media files.
  - o **DynamoDB:** A fast and flexible NoSQL database service for all applications that need consistent, low-latency data access.
- **When to Use:** AWS is great for building large-scale web and mobile apps that require reliable infrastructure, complex backend services, and global scalability.

2. Microsoft Azure:

- **Overview:** Microsoft Azure is a cloud platform offering a wide range of services for building, testing, deploying, and managing applications. Azure is particularly popular among enterprises and companies that rely on Microsoft's ecosystem.

- **Key Services for App Development:**
    - **Azure App Service:** A platform for hosting web applications, RESTful APIs, and mobile backends. It supports multiple languages like .NET, Java, Node.js, Python, and more.
    - **Azure Functions:** A serverless compute service that allows you to run code in response to events such as HTTP requests or messages from a queue.
    - **Azure Blob Storage:** A storage service for unstructured data such as text and binary data, which can be used to store images, video, and backups.
    - **Cosmos DB:** A globally distributed, multi-model database that can be used for high-performance, scalable, and highly available data storage.

- **When to Use:** Azure is ideal for enterprise applications, especially those already using Microsoft technologies (e.g., .NET, SQL Server, and Windows-based environments).

3. Google Cloud Platform (GCP):

- **Overview:** Google Cloud is a cloud platform known for its high-performance computing and machine learning capabilities. It is ideal for apps that require real-time processing, analytics, and advanced data handling.

- **Key Services for App Development:**
  - **Google App Engine:** A fully managed serverless platform for building and deploying web apps and APIs, supporting various languages like Java, Python, Go, Node.js, and more.
  - **Google Cloud Functions:** A serverless compute service that runs code in response to HTTP requests, database changes, or events from cloud services.
  - **Cloud Storage:** Object storage for storing and serving media files, backups, and logs. It's ideal for handling large amounts of data.
  - **Firestore/BigQuery:** Firestore is a NoSQL database, and BigQuery is a data warehouse for handling massive amounts of data. Both are used for scalable storage and real-time data querying.

- **When to Use:** Google Cloud is excellent for applications that require data-intensive operations, analytics, machine learning, and real-time data processing.

Leveraging Cloud for Cross-Platform App Backend

Using cloud services for your app's backend can simplify scaling, storage, and performance management. Here are some common strategies for leveraging cloud platforms for cross-platform app development:

1. Backend-as-a-Service (BaaS):

Cloud platforms like **Firebase (Google Cloud)**, **AWS Amplify**, and **Azure Mobile Apps** offer Backend-as-a-Service (BaaS), which provides ready-made solutions for user authentication, real-time databases, push notifications, and more. These services can save time and reduce complexity when building the backend for cross-platform mobile or web apps.

- **Firebase (Google Cloud):** Firebase offers a suite of tools for building cross-platform apps, including a **real-time database** (Firestore), **Firebase**

Authentication, and **Firebase Cloud Messaging** for push notifications.

Example:

- o You can use **Firebase Authentication** to handle user sign-ins with various methods (email/password, Google, Facebook, etc.), and store data in **Firestore**, a scalable NoSQL database.
- o Firebase offers seamless integration with **Flutter** for building cross-platform mobile apps, making it an ideal choice for mobile developers.

- **AWS Amplify:** AWS Amplify simplifies the process of connecting a frontend app (like React, Angular, or iOS/Android) with AWS services. It includes tools for user authentication, storage (S3), real-time data with **AWS AppSync**, and serverless functions with **AWS Lambda**.

Example:

- o An app built with **React Native** can use **Amplify's Authentication** to handle user registration and sign-in, while **Amplify's API** can connect to **AWS AppSync** to manage real-time data synchronization.

161

2. Using Cloud Functions for Serverless Computing:

Instead of maintaining a full backend server, you can use **serverless computing** to run backend logic on-demand. This allows you to focus on writing the logic without worrying about provisioning servers.

- **AWS Lambda:** Automatically runs your backend code in response to events (e.g., API requests, file uploads) without the need to provision or manage servers.
- **Azure Functions:** A serverless computing service that lets you run code in response to HTTP requests, timers, or events from other services.
- **Google Cloud Functions:** Similarly, Google Cloud Functions can be used to execute backend logic when specific events (like HTTP requests or storage changes) occur.

Serverless computing is ideal for mobile apps with unpredictable or fluctuating traffic because it automatically scales based on demand.

3. Scalable Data Storage and Management:

Cloud platforms provide scalable databases and storage solutions that are essential for apps that handle large amounts of data, user-generated content, or real-time updates.

- **AWS S3 (Simple Storage Service):** Ideal for storing user-uploaded files like images and videos. S3 can scale to handle millions of files and provide high availability.

- **Google Cloud Firestore:** A real-time, scalable NoSQL database perfect for apps that require real-time data synchronization, such as chat applications or collaborative tools.

- **Azure Cosmos DB:** A globally distributed database for managing data with low-latency and high-availability, which is suitable for apps that need to serve global users.

4. APIs and Microservices:

Cloud platforms provide tools for building APIs and microservices, which can be consumed by your cross-platform app. Using tools like **AWS API Gateway**, **Azure API Management**, and **Google Cloud Endpoints**, you can easily create, manage, and deploy APIs that interface with your app.

- **AWS API Gateway:** A fully managed service for creating RESTful APIs that integrate with AWS Lambda or EC2.
- **Azure API Management:** A service for creating and publishing APIs, with built-in tools for monitoring, securing, and analyzing API usage.

Real-World Examples of Cloud-Based Apps

1. **Instagram (AWS):**
   o **Cloud Services Used:** Instagram uses **AWS** to handle its massive traffic, leveraging services like **S3** for media storage and **EC2** instances for compute capacity. Instagram's cloud architecture is highly scalable, allowing it to serve millions of users worldwide with low latency.

2. **WhatsApp (Google Cloud):**
   o **Cloud Services Used:** WhatsApp relies heavily on **Google Cloud** for real-time message processing. The app's backend infrastructure is powered by Google's **App Engine** and **Cloud Pub/Sub** to manage real-time communication and message queues across millions of users.

3. **Spotify (Google Cloud):**

o **Cloud Services Used:** Spotify uses **Google Cloud** for various backend services, including real-time streaming, storage, and data analysis. The company uses **Google Cloud Storage** for media files and **BigQuery** for large-scale data analytics.

4. **Airbnb (AWS and Google Cloud):**

   o **Cloud Services Used:** Airbnb uses a combination of **AWS** and **Google Cloud** for hosting their platform. They leverage **AWS EC2** for compute power and **Google Cloud's BigQuery** for analyzing user data. Additionally, they use **Cloud Storage** for media files and **API Gateway** for their backend APIs.

5. **Netflix (AWS):**

   o **Cloud Services Used:** Netflix is known for its use of **AWS** to handle its massive global user base. Netflix uses **AWS EC2** instances for its streaming infrastructure and **S3** for storing videos. Additionally, they use **AWS Lambda** for processing video data and **CloudFront** for content delivery.

Summary

Cloud platforms like **AWS**, **Azure**, and **Google Cloud** provide a robust set of services that enable developers to build, scale, and maintain powerful cross-platform applications. By leveraging these cloud services, you can focus on building the frontend of your app while relying on the cloud for backend infrastructure, storage, and real-time data synchronization.

Real-world examples from companies like **Instagram**, **WhatsApp**, **Spotify**, and **Airbnb** demonstrate how cloud services can be effectively used to power cross-platform apps, ensuring high performance, scalability, and reliability. Whether you're building a mobile app, web app, or enterprise solution, using cloud platforms will give you the tools to manage your app's backend and ensure it meets user needs across various platforms.

CHAPTER 16

INTEGRATING MACHINE LEARNING AND AI INTO CROSS-PLATFORM APPS

As machine learning (ML) and artificial intelligence (AI) continue to evolve, integrating these technologies into cross-platform apps is becoming increasingly important. Whether it's for voice recognition, recommendation systems, or image processing, AI can significantly enhance user experiences. In this chapter, we will explore the basics of machine learning in **Python** and **C#**, how to implement AI functionalities like voice recognition, recommendation systems, and image processing, and real-world examples of apps that have integrated AI.

Basics of Machine Learning in Python and C#

1. Machine Learning in Python:

Python is widely recognized as one of the best programming languages for machine learning due to its simplicity and the rich ecosystem of libraries available. Here are some key machine learning libraries used in Python:

- **Scikit-learn:** A popular library for implementing machine learning algorithms such as classification, regression, clustering, and dimensionality reduction.
- **TensorFlow and Keras:** Used for developing deep learning models, often applied in image recognition, natural language processing, and reinforcement learning.
- **PyTorch:** Another deep learning framework widely used for training neural networks.
- **Pandas and NumPy:** These libraries are used for data manipulation and processing before feeding it into machine learning algorithms.

Example (Linear Regression with Scikit-learn):

Here's a simple example of using **Scikit-learn** to implement a linear regression model in Python.

```python
import numpy as np
import pandas as pd
from        sklearn.model_selection        import
train_test_split
from        sklearn.linear_model        import
LinearRegression
```

```
from sklearn.metrics import mean_squared_error

# Sample dataset
data = {'X': [1, 2, 3, 4, 5], 'Y': [1, 4, 9, 16, 25]}
df = pd.DataFrame(data)

# Split the dataset
X = df[['X']]
Y = df['Y']
X_train, X_test, Y_train, Y_test = train_test_split(X, Y, test_size=0.2)

# Create and train the model
model = LinearRegression()
model.fit(X_train, Y_train)

# Predictions and evaluation
Y_pred = model.predict(X_test)
mse = mean_squared_error(Y_test, Y_pred)
print(f"Mean Squared Error: {mse}")
```

2. Machine Learning in C#:

While Python is the go-to language for machine learning, **C#** also supports ML, particularly through the **ML.NET** library. **ML.NET** is an open-source framework that allows you to integrate machine learning into your .NET applications.

- **ML.NET:** A machine learning framework for C# and .NET developers. It includes tools for building custom models for tasks such as classification, regression, recommendation, and more.

Example (Binary Classification with ML.NET):

Here's a simple example of using **ML.NET** to perform binary classification on a dataset.

```csharp
using System;
using Microsoft.ML;
using Microsoft.ML.Data;
using Microsoft.ML.Transforms.Conversion;

public class ModelInput
{
    public float Feature { get; set; }
    public bool Label { get; set; }
}

public class ModelOutput
{
    public float PredictedLabel { get; set; }
}

class Program
```

```
{
    static void Main(string[] args)
    {
        var context = new MLContext();
        var data = new[] {
            new ModelInput { Feature = 1.0f,
Label = true },
            new ModelInput { Feature = 2.0f,
Label = false },
            new ModelInput { Feature = 3.0f,
Label = true }
        };

        var trainData =
context.Data.LoadFromEnumerable(data);

        var pipeline =
context.Transforms.Conversion.MapValueToKey("La
bel")

.Append(context.Transforms.Conversion.MapValueT
oKey("Feature"))

.Append(context.Regression.Trainers.Sdca());

        var model = pipeline.Fit(trainData);

        var prediction =
model.Transform(trainData);
```

171

```
        }
}
```

In this example, we load training data, train a model using the **SDCA (Stochastic Dual Coordinate Ascent)** regression trainer, and make predictions.

Implementing AI Functionalities in Cross-Platform Apps

Here, we will discuss some popular AI functionalities that can be integrated into cross-platform apps.

1. Voice Recognition:

Voice recognition allows users to interact with an app using their voice, improving accessibility and user experience. In both Python and C#, various libraries and APIs enable voice recognition:

- **Python (SpeechRecognition Library):** Python offers the **SpeechRecognition** library, which supports various speech-to-text engines. It can recognize speech from audio files or from the microphone in real-time.

Example:

```python

import speech_recognition as sr

recognizer = sr.Recognizer()

with sr.Microphone() as source:
    print("Say something!")
    audio = recognizer.listen(source)

try:
    print("You         said:        "         +
recognizer.recognize_google(audio))
except sr.UnknownValueError:
    print("Sorry,  I  did  not  understand
that.")
except sr.RequestError:
    print("Could not request results.")
```

- **C# (Microsoft Speech SDK):** In C#, the **Microsoft Cognitive Services Speech SDK** allows for easy integration of voice recognition in apps. The SDK provides both speech-to-text and text-to-speech functionalities.

Example:

```csharp
var speechConfig =
SpeechConfig.FromSubscription("YourSubscr
iptionKey", "YourRegion");
var recognizer = new
SpeechRecognizer(speechConfig);

var result = await
recognizer.RecognizeOnceAsync();
if (result.Reason ==
ResultReason.RecognizedSpeech)
{
    Console.WriteLine($"Recognized:
{result.Text}");
}
else
{
    Console.WriteLine("Speech Recognition
failed.");
}
```

2. Recommendation Systems:

Recommendation systems are used to predict what users might like based on their past behavior, preferences, or other users' behaviors. Both Python and C# offer frameworks to implement recommendation algorithms.

- **Python (Surprise Library):** The **Surprise** library in Python is a powerful tool for building recommendation systems. It offers various algorithms like **KNN** (K-Nearest Neighbors), **SVD** (Singular Value Decomposition), and others for collaborative filtering.

Example (Collaborative Filtering):

python

```python
from surprise import Dataset, Reader
from surprise import SVD
from surprise.model_selection import train_test_split
from surprise import accuracy

# Load data
data = Dataset.load_builtin('ml-100k')
trainset, testset = train_test_split(data, test_size=0.2)

# Use SVD for recommendation
model = SVD()
model.fit(trainset)

predictions = model.test(testset)
accuracy.rmse(predictions)
```

- **C# (ML.NET Recommendation API):** In **ML.NET**, you can use the **Matrix Factorization** algorithm to build a recommendation system. It works well for collaborative filtering tasks, such as movie or product recommendations.

Example:

```csharp
var context = new MLContext();
var data = context.Data.LoadFromTextFile<MovieRating>("data.csv", separatorChar: ',');

var pipeline = context.Recommendation().Trainers.MatrixFactorization("Label", "UserId", "MovieId");
var model = pipeline.Fit(data);
```

3. Image Processing and Computer Vision:

AI-powered image processing allows apps to understand and analyze images. This can be used for tasks like object detection, face recognition, and image classification.

- **Python (OpenCV and TensorFlow): OpenCV** is a widely used library for image processing in Python. You can combine OpenCV with **TensorFlow** or **Keras** to build more advanced computer vision applications such as image classification or object detection.

Example (Face Detection with OpenCV):

```python
python

import cv2

# Load pre-trained Haar Cascade model for
face detection
face_cascade                          =
cv2.CascadeClassifier(cv2.data.haarcascad
es                                    +
'haarcascade_frontalface_default.xml')

# Read image
img = cv2.imread('image.jpg')
gray            =            cv2.cvtColor(img,
cv2.COLOR_BGR2GRAY)

# Detect faces
```

177

```
faces                              =
face_cascade.detectMultiScale(gray,    1.1,
4)

for (x, y, w, h) in faces:
    cv2.rectangle(img, (x, y), (x+w, y+h),
(255, 0, 0), 2)

cv2.imshow('Image', img)
cv2.waitKey(0)
cv2.destroyAllWindows()
```

- **C# (Emgu CV for Computer Vision): Emgu CV** is a C# wrapper for OpenCV that allows you to implement computer vision algorithms within C# applications.

Example:

```
csharp

var    img    =    new    Emgu.CV.Image<Bgr,
byte>("image.jpg");
var grayImg = img.Convert<Gray, byte>();

var        faceCascade        =        new
CascadeClassifier("haarcascade_frontalfac
e_default.xml");
```

178

```
var                    faces                  =
faceCascade.DetectMultiScale(grayImg);

foreach (var face in faces)
{
    img.Draw(face, new Bgr(Color.Red), 2);
}

img.Save("output.jpg");
```

Real-World Examples of Apps with Integrated AI

1. **Google Assistant (Voice Recognition):**

   o **AI Functionality:** Voice recognition allows users to interact with Google Assistant using natural language. The app uses Google's **Speech-to-Text** API to convert speech into text, which is then processed for tasks like setting reminders or controlling smart devices.

2. **Netflix (Recommendation System):**

   o **AI Functionality:** Netflix uses machine learning for its recommendation system. It tracks users' watching habits and suggests content based on their preferences. The system uses collaborative filtering, content-based filtering, and hybrid models.

3. **Face ID on iPhone (Image Processing):**

- o **AI Functionality:** Apple's **Face ID** uses machine learning and computer vision algorithms to recognize a user's face. The app processes facial features using deep learning models and allows secure authentication for unlocking the phone or making payments.

4. **Amazon Alexa (Voice Recognition & AI):**

- o **AI Functionality:** Alexa allows users to interact with devices through voice commands. It uses **natural language processing (NLP)** to understand and respond to voice commands, such as setting timers or controlling smart home devices.

Summary

Integrating AI and machine learning into cross-platform apps can significantly enhance functionality, offering features like voice recognition, recommendation systems, and image processing. Python and C# both provide powerful tools for building and deploying AI models, and leveraging cloud services can simplify the backend integration. Real-world examples like **Google Assistant**, **Netflix**, and **Face ID** showcase the powerful capabilities that AI can bring to cross-platform apps, improving user experience and engagement.

CHAPTER 17

CROSS-PLATFORM DEVELOPMENT FOR IOT (INTERNET OF THINGS)

The Internet of Things (IoT) is transforming the way we interact with the world by connecting everyday objects to the internet, enabling them to send and receive data. Cross-platform development plays a crucial role in building IoT applications that work seamlessly across different devices and platforms. In this chapter, we'll introduce IoT and its relevance to cross-platform apps, explore how to build IoT applications using **Python** and **C#**, and provide real-world examples of successful IoT-based cross-platform apps.

Introduction to IoT and Its Relevance to Cross-Platform Apps

1. What is IoT?

The Internet of Things (IoT) refers to the network of physical devices, vehicles, appliances, and other objects embedded with sensors, software, and other technologies to connect and exchange data with other devices and systems over the internet. These devices can range from household appliances like refrigerators and thermostats to industrial machinery and even wearable devices.

IoT has become a significant driver of innovation, impacting various industries, such as healthcare, manufacturing, agriculture, transportation, and home automation. IoT devices collect real-time data that can be processed and acted upon, creating opportunities for automation, remote monitoring, and data analysis.

2. The Role of Cross-Platform Apps in IoT:

Cross-platform apps are essential in IoT because they enable communication between IoT devices and users, regardless of the platform (e.g., Android, iOS, Windows, or web). By using a single codebase for multiple platforms, developers can reduce development time and ensure a consistent user experience across devices.

Here's why cross-platform development is particularly useful for IoT:

- **Unified User Interface:** Users can interact with multiple IoT devices through a single app on any platform, be it mobile, tablet, or web.

- **Device Interoperability:** Cross-platform apps can communicate with different IoT devices built on various hardware, regardless of whether the device is Android-based, iOS-based, or uses different protocols.

- **Efficient Development:** Writing one app that works across multiple platforms saves time and resources, which is essential in the fast-evolving world of IoT.

Building IoT Applications with Python and C#

1. Building IoT Apps with Python:

Python is widely used in the IoT space due to its simplicity, extensive libraries, and ability to interface with various hardware devices. Many IoT frameworks and libraries in Python make it easy to connect sensors, collect data, and process it.

- **Popular Python Libraries for IoT:**
  - **RPi.GPIO:** A library for controlling the General Purpose Input/Output (GPIO) pins on the **Raspberry Pi**.

- o **Paho MQTT:** A client library for **MQTT**, a popular lightweight messaging protocol used in IoT for real-time communication.
- o **Flask or Django:** These web frameworks can be used to create a web-based interface for controlling IoT devices or visualizing data.

Example: IoT Temperature Monitoring System Using Python

In this example, we'll build a basic temperature monitoring system that collects data from a sensor (such as a **DHT11** temperature and humidity sensor) and sends it to a web interface.

python

```
import Adafruit_DHT
import paho.mqtt.client as mqtt
import time

# Sensor setup
sensor = Adafruit_DHT.DHT11
pin = 4  # GPIO pin where the sensor is connected

# MQTT setup
broker = "mqtt.eclipse.org"
port = 1883
```

```
topic = "home/temperature"

client = mqtt.Client()
client.connect(broker, port, 60)

# Main loop to read temperature data and send via
MQTT
while True:
    humidity,          temperature          =
Adafruit_DHT.read_retry(sensor, pin)

    if temperature is not None:
        print(f"Temperature: {temperature}°C")
        # Publish temperature data to MQTT
        client.publish(topic,      f"Temperature:
{temperature}°C")
    else:
        print("Failed   to   get   reading.   Try
again!")

    time.sleep(5)
```

In this example:

- The **Adafruit_DHT** library is used to interface with the DHT11 sensor, which measures temperature and humidity.
- The **Paho MQTT** library is used to send the temperature data to a cloud broker (like **Eclipse Mosquitto**).

186

This Python script collects data from the sensor and sends it over the internet to be monitored remotely through a cross-platform app.

---

2. Building IoT Apps with C#:

C# is also a popular language for developing IoT applications, especially for Windows-based devices and applications running on the **.NET** ecosystem. C# is frequently used with the **Universal Windows Platform (UWP)**, which allows you to create apps that work across Windows 10 devices, including desktops, smartphones, and IoT devices like Raspberry Pi.

- **Popular C# Libraries for IoT:**
    - **Windows.Devices.Gpio:** A library that allows access to the GPIO pins on a Raspberry Pi or other supported Windows IoT devices.
    - **MQTTnet:** A .NET library that allows you to implement the MQTT protocol for communication between IoT devices and applications.
    - **Azure IoT SDK:** For apps that need to connect to the cloud, **Azure IoT Hub SDK** allows you to

send and receive data from IoT devices to **Microsoft Azure**.

Example: IoT Temperature Monitoring System Using C#

Here's an example where a **Raspberry Pi** running **Windows IoT Core** can collect temperature data and send it to an MQTT broker for remote monitoring.

csharp

```csharp
using System;
using Windows.Devices.Gpio;
using MQTTnet;
using MQTTnet.Client;
using System.Threading.Tasks;

class Program
{
    static async Task Main(string[] args)
    {
        var gpio = GpioController.GetDefault();
        var pin = gpio.OpenPin(17); // GPIO pin
for temperature sensor

pin.SetDriveMode(GpioPinDriveMode.Input);

        var mqttFactory = new MqttFactory();
```

```
        var            mqttClient         =
mqttFactory.CreateMqttClient();
        var        mqttOptions      =        new
MqttClientOptionsBuilder()
            .WithTcpServer("mqtt.eclipse.org")
            .Build();

        await
mqttClient.ConnectAsync(mqttOptions);

        while (true)
        {
            int           temperature        =
GetTemperature(pin);  // Placeholder function for
getting temperature
            string   message   =   $"Temperature:
{temperature}°C";
            var      mqttMessage       =       new
MqttApplicationMessageBuilder()
                .WithTopic("home/temperature")
                .WithPayload(message)
                .Build();

        await
mqttClient.PublishAsync(mqttMessage);
            Console.WriteLine(message);
            await Task.Delay(5000);
        }
    }
```

189

```
static int GetTemperature(GpioPin pin)
{
    // Simulate reading temperature (replace
with actual sensor reading logic)
    return new Random().Next(15, 30);
}
}
```

In this C# example:

- The **Windows.Devices.Gpio** library is used to interact with the GPIO pins on the Raspberry Pi.
- The **MQTTnet** library is used to send temperature data to an MQTT broker, similar to the Python example.

This approach allows you to create IoT applications that can interface with sensors and cloud services, integrating seamlessly into cross-platform apps.

Real-World Examples of IoT-Based Cross-Platform Apps

1. **Nest Thermostat (Home Automation):**
   o **Technology Used:** The **Nest Thermostat** allows users to control their home's heating and cooling systems remotely. The app can run on multiple

platforms (iOS, Android, and web), communicating with the Nest thermostat using IoT protocols like **MQTT**.

- o **How It Works:** Users can adjust their home temperature through a cross-platform app, which sends commands to the thermostat over the internet. The device collects data on usage patterns, learning when the user prefers different temperatures and optimizing for energy savings.

2. **Smart Home Devices (Amazon Alexa, Google Assistant):**

   - o **Technology Used:** Amazon **Alexa** and **Google Assistant** are IoT platforms that allow users to control smart home devices via voice commands. These devices integrate with various IoT protocols, such as **Z-Wave** and **Zigbee**, and provide cross-platform support across smartphones, tablets, and smart speakers.

   - o **How It Works:** Alexa or Google Assistant collects data from smart sensors (e.g., temperature sensors, motion detectors), processes the information, and allows users to interact with the devices via cross-platform apps. These apps are built using frameworks like **React Native** or **Flutter**.

3. **Fitbit (Wearable Devices):**

- o **Technology Used: Fitbit** integrates IoT sensors in wearable devices that track user activity, heart rate, sleep patterns, and more. The Fitbit app is available on iOS, Android, and web platforms, providing cross-platform access to the data.

- o **How It Works:** The wearable device sends sensor data to the cloud through Bluetooth or Wi-Fi. The Fitbit app uses this data to track the user's health and fitness, providing insights and recommendations for a healthier lifestyle.

4. **Smart Farming (IoT Sensors in Agriculture):**

- o **Technology Used:** Smart farming solutions use IoT devices to monitor soil moisture, temperature, and other environmental factors to optimize farming practices. These systems use sensors deployed in the field to collect data and make decisions about irrigation, planting, and harvesting.

- o **How It Works:** The collected data is sent to the cloud, where it's analyzed and used to send real-time recommendations to farmers via a cross-platform app. This app might run on mobile devices or web browsers, and it communicates with IoT devices using protocols like **MQTT** or **CoAP**.

Summary

Integrating IoT with cross-platform apps opens up endless possibilities for enhancing user experiences and creating innovative solutions. Python and C# offer robust libraries and tools for working with IoT devices, enabling developers to build everything from smart home systems to wearable health trackers. Real-world examples like **Nest Thermostat**, **Amazon Alexa**, **Fitbit**, and **Smart Farming** demonstrate the impact of IoT-based cross-platform apps in various industries, showcasing how IoT can streamline processes, optimize resources, and improve user engagement.

CHAPTER 18

ADVANCED TOPICS IN CROSS-PLATFORM DEVELOPMENT

As cross-platform development evolves, developers face increasingly complex challenges and the need for advanced techniques to create highly efficient, scalable, and maintainable apps. This chapter explores advanced concepts like concurrency and asynchronous programming, the use of design patterns, and real-world examples of advanced development techniques that help optimize cross-platform applications.

Advanced Concepts: Concurrency and Asynchronous Programming

1. Concurrency:

Concurrency refers to the ability of an app to perform multiple tasks at the same time. It doesn't necessarily mean tasks are executed simultaneously (that's parallelism), but that tasks are managed so they can overlap, allowing more efficient use of system resources. In a cross-platform context, managing concurrency effectively is critical for handling I/O operations, network requests, and user interface updates without blocking the main thread.

- **Threads and Task Scheduling:** In cross-platform apps, tasks like network requests, file reading, or database operations should run in the background to prevent freezing the user interface (UI). Both **Python** and **C#** offer libraries and tools for managing concurrency.

  o **Python:**

    ▪ **Threading:** The `threading` module provides a way to run multiple threads simultaneously. However, Python's **Global Interpreter Lock (GIL)** limits true parallelism in CPU-bound tasks but allows concurrency in I/O-bound tasks.

    ▪ **Asyncio:** Python's `asyncio` library allows for asynchronous programming, where code can be non-blocking and perform other tasks while waiting for I/O operations.

  Example (Python threading):

195

```
python

import threading
import time

def print_numbers():
    for i in range(10):
        print(i)
        time.sleep(1)

thread                            =
threading.Thread(target=print_numbers)
thread.start()
thread.join()  # Wait for thread to finish
```

- o **C#:**
  - ▪ **Task Parallel Library (TPL):** The TPL simplifies working with asynchronous and parallel code in C#. The `Task` class and `async/await` keywords allow you to write asynchronous code that is easy to manage.

Example (C# async/await):

```csharp
csharp

using System;
using System.Threading.Tasks;
```

```
public class Program
{
    public static async Task Main(string[]
args)
    {
        Console.WriteLine("Start");
        await PrintNumbersAsync();
        Console.WriteLine("End");
    }

    public     static     async     Task
PrintNumbersAsync()
    {
        for (int i = 0; i < 10; i++)
        {
            Console.WriteLine(i);
            await  Task.Delay(1000);     //
Non-blocking delay
        }
    }
}
```

2. Asynchronous Programming:

Asynchronous programming allows a program to perform tasks without blocking its execution. It's essential for tasks that involve waiting, such as network requests or file operations, as it prevents freezing or blocking the user interface.

- **Python's Asyncio:** With `asyncio`, Python developers can create asynchronous code that handles I/O-bound tasks without waiting for operations like database queries or API calls to complete before moving on to the next task.
- **C# Async/Await:** C# provides powerful tools for asynchronous programming using the `async` and `await` keywords. This makes writing asynchronous code as straightforward as synchronous code, allowing developers to handle I/O-bound operations without blocking the main thread.

Asynchronous programming improves performance by ensuring that the application remains responsive, even when performing time-consuming tasks.

Using Design Patterns in Cross-Platform Apps

Design patterns are proven solutions to common design problems in software development. In cross-platform development, design patterns can help improve code structure, maintainability, and reusability.

1. Model-View-ViewModel (MVVM):

The MVVM pattern is commonly used in cross-platform apps (especially in frameworks like Xamarin and **.NET MAUI**) to separate the user interface (View) from the business logic and data (Model). The **ViewModel** acts as an intermediary, exposing data and commands in a way that the View can bind to without directly coupling with the Model.

- **View:** Represents the UI components that the user interacts with.
- **ViewModel:** Acts as a bridge, providing the data for the View and accepting user input, but contains no logic for rendering.
- **Model:** Contains the app's core data and business logic.

Example (MVVM in C# with Xamarin):

csharp

```csharp
public class MainPageViewModel
{
    public string Name { get; set; }
    public ICommand ButtonClickCommand { get; }
```

```
public MainPageViewModel()
{
    ButtonClickCommand          =          new
Command(OnButtonClick);
}

private void OnButtonClick()
{
    Name = "Hello, Xamarin!";
}
}
```

In this example, the **ViewModel** contains the business logic and the properties bound to the **View**. The **Model** would contain any data-related functionality.

2. Singleton Pattern:

The **Singleton Pattern** ensures that a class has only one instance and provides a global point of access to it. This is especially useful in cross-platform apps where you need to maintain a single instance of a service (e.g., network manager, logging service, or database connection) throughout the app.

- **Python Example:**

python

```python
class Singleton:
    _instance = None

    def __new__(cls):
        if cls._instance is None:
            cls._instance  =  super(Singleton,
cls).__new__(cls)
        return cls._instance

# Usage
singleton1 = Singleton()
singleton2 = Singleton()
print(singleton1 is singleton2)  # True
```

- **C# Example:**

csharp

```csharp
public class Singleton
{
    private static Singleton _instance;
    private static readonly object _lock = new
object();

    private Singleton() { }

    public static Singleton Instance
    {
```

```
get
{
    lock (_lock)
    {
        if (_instance == null)
        {
            _instance = new Singleton();
        }
        return _instance;
    }
}
}
```

The Singleton pattern ensures that you have only one instance of the class, making it easy to manage shared resources or configurations across the app.

3. Observer Pattern:

The **Observer Pattern** allows objects (observers) to subscribe to and receive notifications from another object (the subject) when its state changes. This pattern is especially useful for building responsive, event-driven user interfaces.

In cross-platform apps, the **Observer Pattern** is commonly used for updating the UI based on changes in the application's state or data (e.g., data binding in MVVM).

Example in C#:

```csharp
public class EventPublisher
{
    public event EventHandler DataChanged;

    public void Notify()
    {
        DataChanged?.Invoke(this,
EventArgs.Empty);
    }
}

public class EventListener
{
    public void OnDataChanged(object sender,
EventArgs e)
    {
        Console.WriteLine("Data has changed!");
    }
}
```

Real-World Examples of Advanced Development Techniques

1. Real-Time Collaboration (Google Docs):

- **Technology Used:** Google Docs leverages real-time collaboration using websockets and the **Observer Pattern**. When one user makes a change, other users instantly see it. Asynchronous programming is used to handle simultaneous editing without blocking the user interface.

- **Advanced Techniques:** Google Docs uses the **MVVM** pattern for managing the separation of concerns in its codebase, allowing updates to the document (Model) to be reflected in real time in the UI (View), using the ViewModel as the intermediary.

2. Spotify (Music Streaming):

- **Technology Used:** Spotify uses a combination of **asynchronous programming** for streaming music, **Observer Pattern** for updating the UI based on user interactions, and **Singleton Pattern** for managing the audio service throughout the app.

- **Advanced Techniques:** Spotify handles concurrent network requests using **Task Parallel Library (TPL)** and ensures smooth playback by managing threads and processes efficiently.

3. Airbnb (Vacation Rental Platform):

- **Technology Used:** Airbnb uses **MVVM** for managing data in its cross-platform mobile apps. The app updates the UI in real time as users search for properties or book rentals, ensuring a smooth user experience.

- **Advanced Techniques:** Airbnb also uses **Singleton Pattern** for managing user sessions and network requests efficiently, ensuring data consistency across the app.

Summary

Advanced topics in cross-platform development, such as concurrency, asynchronous programming, and the application of design patterns, are essential for building efficient, scalable, and maintainable apps. By mastering these techniques, developers can create apps that handle multiple tasks seamlessly, provide smooth user experiences, and remain adaptable as the app evolves.

The integration of design patterns like **MVVM, Singleton,** and **Observer**, combined with the powerful capabilities of asynchronous and concurrent programming, ensures that your app can scale, perform optimally, and maintain a high-quality user experience across all platforms. Real-world examples from apps like **Google Docs**, **Spotify**, and **Airbnb** show how these advanced techniques can be applied to solve complex challenges in cross-platform development.

CHAPTER 19

THE FUTURE OF CROSS-PLATFORM DEVELOPMENT

Cross-platform development has come a long way, but it is far from stagnant. As technology continues to evolve, new trends and tools are shaping the future of cross-platform apps. This chapter explores emerging trends and technologies in cross-platform development, what's next for **Python**, **C#**, and cross-platform frameworks, and how developers can prepare for the future of app development.

Emerging Trends and Technologies in Cross-Platform Development

1. Increased Focus on Unified Platforms:

Unified cross-platform frameworks that allow developers to write code once and deploy it to a variety of platforms are becoming more sophisticated. **Flutter**, **React Native**, and **Xamarin** are leading the charge in this space, but the future promises even more improvements in these frameworks, offering better performance, ease of use, and more native-like user experiences.

- **Flutter (Dart):** Google's **Flutter** has gained immense popularity due to its ability to provide high performance across platforms while offering a rich set of pre-built widgets for a native look and feel. In the future, expect more tools and features that allow Flutter to extend beyond mobile and into desktop and web apps more seamlessly.

- **React Native:** Facebook's **React Native** continues to be a dominant player in cross-platform development, especially for mobile apps. The trend toward enhanced **performance** through tools like **Hermes** (a JavaScript engine) and better **native module integration** is making React Native more efficient.

- **.NET MAUI:** **.NET MAUI** (Multi-platform App UI) is an evolution of Xamarin that allows you to build apps for Android, iOS, macOS, and Windows with a single codebase. With **.NET MAUI**, we can expect better support for modern UI controls and deeper integration with **.NET 6+**.

2. AI and Machine Learning Integration:

As artificial intelligence (AI) and machine learning (ML) become more integral to user experiences, cross-platform development frameworks will increasingly integrate with AI and ML services. The ability to build smarter apps that can learn from user behavior and automate tasks is one of the most significant trends in modern app development.

- **AI-Enhanced User Interfaces:** Expect to see more apps with intelligent UIs that adapt to user preferences. This could include recommendations, personalized experiences, and predictive inputs.
- **Integration with Cloud AI Services:** Cross-platform apps will increasingly integrate with **cloud-based AI services** (e.g., **Google Cloud AI**, **AWS AI services**, and **Microsoft Azure Cognitive Services**) to add features like voice recognition, image processing, and natural language understanding.

3. Real-Time Collaboration and Connectivity:

With the rise of remote work and collaboration, real-time functionality in cross-platform apps will be a growing focus. Features like live document editing, chat, and video calls will continue to improve.

- **WebSockets & Real-Time Data Syncing:** WebSockets, combined with real-time database solutions like **Firebase** or **AWS AppSync**, will power collaborative apps by enabling fast, bidirectional communication between the app and its backend.

- **Progressive Web Apps (PWAs):** PWAs are gaining traction because they offer the best of both web and mobile apps, allowing users to install apps directly from the web. They also have the potential to enable real-time collaboration without requiring the user to download a dedicated app.

4. Progressive Web Apps (PWAs) and Edge Computing:

As we move toward more distributed app architectures, **edge computing** will enable IoT devices and PWAs to perform processing tasks at the edge of the network (closer to the user) instead of relying entirely on cloud servers. This improves performance, reduces latency, and enhances user experience.

- **PWAs for Cross-Platform Development:** PWAs are becoming a key trend for apps that need to be deployed across multiple platforms with minimal overhead. They work on both mobile and desktop platforms, offering offline capabilities, push notifications, and access to device hardware, which makes them a cost-effective solution for building cross-platform apps.

What's Next for Python, C#, and Cross-Platform Frameworks

1. What's Next for Python:

Python continues to be a top choice for many developers, especially in data science, machine learning, and backend development. As Python matures, the language will likely become even more integrated into cross-platform development, especially with frameworks like **Kivy**, **PyQt**, and **BeeWare**. However, Python's lack of native mobile support has driven the rise of other tools to bridge this gap.

- **Kivy and BeeWare:** While Python is not traditionally used for mobile development, frameworks like **Kivy** and **BeeWare** are paving the way for cross-platform mobile apps. These tools allow Python developers to create apps that can run on iOS, Android, and even desktop environments.
- **Python for IoT:** Python is a dominant language for Internet of Things (IoT) development. Expect to see increased usage of Python in IoT, with cross-

platform frameworks providing easy integration with a wide variety of IoT devices.

- **Python in Cloud and Serverless Computing:** Python's flexibility in cloud-based environments, especially with **AWS Lambda**, **Google Cloud Functions**, and **Azure Functions**, will lead to more cloud-native, cross-platform applications leveraging Python for microservices and serverless functions.

2. What's Next for C#:

C# and .NET are continuing to evolve, and the **.NET 6** and **.NET MAUI** updates have enhanced C#'s position in the cross-platform space. **.NET MAUI** will allow for seamless cross-platform development on mobile, desktop, and web from a single codebase.

- **.NET MAUI:** Building on Xamarin's legacy, **.NET MAUI** extends cross-platform support to desktop and web apps while simplifying the development process. Expect **better UI components**, **performance optimizations**, and **cross-platform integrations** (including APIs for modern hardware features).

- **C# for Web and Cloud:** As C# continues to grow, we'll see it become a more prominent language in **cloud-native development**, especially with the rise of **Azure** and **AWS** cloud services. C# developers can leverage **Azure Functions** and **AWS Lambda** for serverless computing, helping them create scalable, event-driven applications.

- **C# in Gaming: Unity**, a popular game development engine, uses C# as its primary language. The growing gaming industry, especially mobile games and VR/AR, will push for even more cross-platform development support from C#.

3. What's Next for Cross-Platform Frameworks:

- **Flutter's Growth: Flutter** has grown in popularity due to its performance advantages, especially in mobile app development. With the addition of desktop support and better tooling, **Flutter** could become the go-to framework for building apps across all platforms.

- **React Native: React Native** will continue to dominate mobile development, especially with the enhancements around **React Native Web** and more seamless integration with native code, giving

213

developers the flexibility to add custom native modules when needed.

- **.NET MAUI and Xamarin:** The next step for **.NET MAUI** is to offer unified support for Android, iOS, Windows, and macOS from a single codebase, positioning it as a compelling option for **C#** developers building apps for multiple platforms.

Preparing for the Future of App Development

As we look to the future of cross-platform development, there are a few key strategies that developers can use to stay ahead of the curve:

1. **Stay Up-to-Date with Emerging Frameworks:**
   o Keep an eye on emerging frameworks like **Flutter, React Native,** and **.NET MAUI** as they continue to evolve and become more powerful.
   o Invest time in learning the **native development languages** (Java, Swift, Kotlin) for deeper customization when necessary.
2. **Master Cloud Integration:**
   o With the increased importance of cloud computing, cloud-native development, and serverless architectures, it's essential for

214

developers to understand how to integrate cloud services (AWS, Azure, Google Cloud) with cross-platform apps.

3. **Leverage AI and ML:**

   o AI is becoming a core part of mobile and web applications. Be prepared to integrate machine learning models into apps, using frameworks like **TensorFlow**, **PyTorch**, or **ML.NET** to create intelligent apps.

4. **Embrace the Internet of Things (IoT):**

   o As IoT continues to grow, gaining knowledge in IoT development, especially for cross-platform applications, will be essential for building smart apps that interact with a variety of connected devices.

5. **Prioritize User-Centric Design:**

   o As more platforms emerge and user expectations continue to rise, maintaining a strong focus on user experience (UX) design is crucial. Invest in creating **responsive**, **intuitive**, and **accessible** designs for a diverse range of users.

6. **Adapt to Real-Time and Collaborative Apps:**

   o Real-time collaboration features (like in **Google Docs** and **Slack**) are becoming standard in many applications. Whether you're developing social apps, messaging services, or collaboration tools, mastering the technologies that enable real-time data syncing and communication is crucial.

Summary

The future of cross-platform development is bright, with emerging technologies, frameworks, and trends shaping the way we build and deploy applications. As developers, it's essential to stay informed about the evolution of frameworks like **Flutter**, **React Native**, and **.NET MAUI**, while also mastering new areas like **AI**, **machine learning**, **cloud computing**, and **IoT**.

By embracing these advancements and staying adaptable, developers can ensure they're ready to tackle the challenges of the future and continue creating high-performing, scalable, and user-friendly cross-platform applications across all devices and platforms.

CHAPTER 20

FINAL THOUGHTS AND NEXT STEPS

As we conclude this journey through cross-platform development, it's important to reflect on the key concepts you've learned and how to continue your path toward mastering cross-platform technologies. In this chapter, we'll recap the important takeaways from the book, suggest ways to continue learning, and provide actionable tips for applying your skills in the real world, along with strategies for ongoing growth in the tech industry.

Recap of Key Concepts Learned Throughout the Book

1. Cross-Platform Development:

- **What it is:** Cross-platform development enables you to create applications that run on multiple platforms (iOS, Android, Windows, Web, etc.) using a single codebase, saving time, effort, and resources.

- **Why it matters:** It's crucial for building apps that reach a broad user base while maintaining efficiency and ensuring consistency across different devices.

2. Frameworks and Tools:

- **Flutter, React Native, Xamarin, and .NET MAUI:** We explored the most popular cross-platform frameworks, each offering unique features for mobile and desktop development. These frameworks allow you to build high-performance applications with a unified codebase.
- **Python, C#, and .NET Core:** We discussed how **Python** and **C#** can be used in cross-platform development, with specific libraries and frameworks for building apps that work seamlessly across various platforms.

3. Advanced Topics in Cross-Platform Development:

- **Concurrency and Asynchronous Programming:** These techniques help in creating responsive, efficient apps by managing background tasks and preventing UI blocking.
- **Design Patterns:** We looked at patterns like **MVVM**, **Singleton**, and **Observer** that help in maintaining clean, scalable, and reusable code.
- **AI and Machine Learning Integration:** We explored how to add AI and machine learning capabilities to cross-

platform apps, from voice recognition to recommendation systems and image processing.

- **IoT Integration:** We learned how IoT devices interact with cross-platform apps, expanding app capabilities in industries like home automation, healthcare, and industrial monitoring.

4. Cloud Services and APIs:

- We discussed the importance of cloud platforms like **AWS**, **Azure**, and **Google Cloud** in modern app development, covering how they help in scaling, storing data, and adding powerful backends for IoT, machine learning, and real-time collaboration features.

5. Real-World Application:

- We examined real-world examples like **Spotify**, **Google Docs**, and **Nest Thermostat**, which have successfully leveraged cross-platform development and advanced technologies to enhance user experience, scalability, and functionality.

How to Continue Learning and Improving Your Cross-Platform Development Skills

1. Stay Up to Date with New Technologies:

- The tech industry evolves quickly, and so do cross-platform frameworks. Follow blogs, attend conferences, and participate in webinars to keep up with the latest trends and updates in cross-platform development.
- Some great resources include **Dev.to**, **Stack Overflow**, **GitHub**, and official documentation for frameworks like **Flutter**, **React Native**, **Xamarin**, and **.NET MAUI**.

2. Contribute to Open Source:

- Contributing to open-source projects is a great way to deepen your knowledge, collaborate with other developers, and give back to the community. It also provides practical experience with real-world projects.
- Platforms like **GitHub** offer many opportunities to contribute to open-source cross-platform development tools, libraries, and apps.

3. Work on Personal Projects:

- Continuously practice by building your own cross-platform apps. Choose real-world problems and create apps to solve them, whether it's a weather app, a to-do list, or something more advanced like a home automation system.

- By creating diverse projects, you will gain hands-on experience and uncover unique challenges that will help you learn and improve.

4. Expand Your Knowledge with Online Courses:

- Online platforms like **Udemy, Coursera, edX**, and **Pluralsight** offer courses on cross-platform development, AI, cloud computing, and other technologies relevant to the field.
- You can take specific courses on advanced topics such as **Flutter for Web, React Native, .NET MAUI**, or **Machine Learning with TensorFlow** to deepen your expertise.

Tips for Real-World Application and Continued Growth in the Tech Industry

1. Focus on User-Centered Development:

- In the real world, the goal of cross-platform development is not just to build an app that works on multiple platforms, but to build one that users love. Always prioritize the user experience (UX) and user interface (UI) design, ensuring your app is intuitive, responsive, and accessible.

- Test your app extensively on different devices and platforms to guarantee a seamless user experience.

2. Collaborate with Cross-Disciplinary Teams:

- Modern development often involves working with teams of backend developers, designers, product managers, and other stakeholders. Be prepared to collaborate effectively, communicating ideas clearly and working in an agile, iterative development process.
- Learn to understand the requirements and constraints of other team members to build better, more cohesive apps.

3. Build a Strong Portfolio:

- Create a portfolio showcasing your best work, whether it's personal projects, contributions to open-source, or apps you've developed in a team setting. A portfolio is a tangible way to demonstrate your skills and attract potential employers or clients.
- Include a variety of projects that demonstrate your ability to work with different cross-platform frameworks, tackle complex problems, and implement advanced features like AI and IoT.

4. Network and Engage with the Developer Community:

- Join online communities such as **Reddit**, **Stack Overflow**, and **Twitter** to discuss ideas, ask questions, and share knowledge. Engaging with the community allows you to learn from others, discover new tools, and stay motivated.
- Consider attending meetups, conferences, and hackathons to build connections, find mentorship, and learn from industry experts.

5. Continuously Refine Your Skills:

- Always be ready to learn, iterate, and grow. The tech industry is fast-paced, and developers who are adaptable and continuously improving their skill set stand out.
- Make it a habit to regularly practice coding, learn new frameworks, and take on challenges that push you out of your comfort zone. Explore adjacent areas like **DevOps**, **cloud computing**, or **cybersecurity** to broaden your expertise.

This book has covered the core concepts, frameworks, and advanced topics in cross-platform development, giving you a solid foundation for building efficient, scalable, and high-quality apps across multiple platforms. As the tech landscape evolves, the ability to adapt, learn new technologies, and apply them in real-world projects will be essential to your continued success as a developer.

By staying updated with emerging technologies, working on diverse projects, collaborating with teams, and expanding your knowledge, you'll continue to grow as a developer and position yourself for long-term success in the ever-evolving tech industry. The future of cross-platform development is bright, and with the skills you've gained, you are well-equipped to be a part of that future.

www.ingramcontent.com/pod-product-compliance
Lightning Source LLC
LaVergne TN
LVHW051324050326
832903LV00031B/3345